BALDRIGE

20|20

An Executive's Guide to the Criteria for Performance Excellence

With Forewords by
Rosabeth Moss Kanter
and Gregory R. Page

Featuring Data and Stories from Organizations
That Used the Criteria to Become U.S. Role Models

Baldrige Performance Excellence Program
National Institute of Standards and Technology
U.S. Department of Commerce
100 Bureau Drive, Stop 1020
Gaithersburg, MD 20899-1020
Telephone: (301) 975-2036 • Fax: (301) 948-3716
E-Mail: baldrige@nist.gov • Web Site: http://www.nist.gov/baldrige

Printed in August 2011 in the United States of America

Lead author: Christine Schaefer; lead editor: Dawn Bailey. The following staff members of the Baldrige Performance Excellence Program also contributed to this publication: Marilyn Barstow, Jacqueline Calhoun, Ellen Garshick, Millie Glick, Harry Hertz, Scott Kurtz, and Jeff Lucas. Book design and illustrations by Capitol Communication Systems, Inc., Crofton, MD

The Baldrige Program gratefully acknowledges the Baldrige Award winners whose stories, figures/data, and photos appear in this book: AtlantiCare; Boeing Mobility; Cargill Corn Milling; City of Coral Springs; DM Petroleum Operations Company; Freese and Nichols Inc.; Heartland Health; Honeywell Federal Manufacturing and Technologies, L.L.C.; Iredell-Statesville Schools; MEDRAD, Inc.; Mercy Health System; MESA Products, Inc.; MidwayUSA; Montgomery County Public Schools; Nestlé Purina PetCare Company; Poudre Valley Health System; Premier Inc.; PRO-TEC Coating Company; Richland College; The Ritz-Carlton Hotel Company, L.L.C.; Sharp HealthCare; SSM Health Care; Texas Nameplate Company, Inc.; U.S. Army Armament Research, Development and Engineering Center; and Veterans Affairs Cooperative Studies Program Clinical Research Pharmacy Coordinating Center.

Cover photos: Top row, clockwise: Terry Holliday, former superintendent, Iredell-Statesville Schools; Quint Studer, CEO and founder, Studer Group; Joseph King, former chief human capital officer, U.S. Army Armament Research, Development and Engineering Center; Sister Mary Jean Ryan, FSM, president and CEO, SSM Health Care; David Tilton, CEO, AtlantiCare; Samuel M. Liang, president and CEO, Medrad; Mike Sather, director, Veterans Affairs Cooperative Studies Program Clinical Research Pharmacy Coordinating Center; and JoAnn Brumit, CEO, KARLEE

The National Institute of Standards and Technology is not recommending or endorsing the organizations featured in this book. Organizational results referenced in this publication reflect current data at the time each organization received the Malcolm Baldrige National Quality Award.

For more information on the Baldrige Criteria for Performance Excellence and the Malcolm Baldrige National Quality Award, visit http://www.nist.gov/baldrige/. For more information on state, local, and sector-specific awards based on the Baldrige Criteria, visit the Alliance for Performance for Excellence at http://www.baldrigepe.org/alliance/.

Contents

Foreword

by Rosabeth Moss Kanter

The Malcolm Baldrige National Quality Award (as the Baldrige Program was first known) was developed in response to a crisis in U.S. competitiveness several decades ago, at the dawn of the global information era. American manufacturing was losing ground to Japanese companies which had adopted quality improvement systems taught to them, ironically, by an American, W. Edwards Deming, as part of the rebuilding effort after World War II. The Deming Prize was named in his honor in 1950 in Japan. By the mid-1980s, Japan was an economic powerhouse, and sluggish U.S. companies were under pressure to seek performance excellence and innovation or risk losing further ground. The rise of Japanese industry, from automotive manufacturing to electronics, could not be written off as due to low-cost labor; it was clearly seen as emanating from outstanding management systems, captured in the criteria for the Deming Prize.

In 1987, the U.S. government countered with its own prize, the Baldrige Award, to encourage American companies to examine their practices, benchmark against the best companies, and make necessary changes to become leaner, faster, and more customer-oriented, with fact-based decisions and responsiveness to multiple stakeholders, all in pursuit of zero defects and high performance. This quest for quality, backed by a prize awarded by the President of the United States, became a national movement, informing management practices well beyond the companies applying for the prize. The success of the Baldrige program in stimulating change led its leaders to apply it to other major sectors requiring transformation, notably health care and education. I was privileged to serve on the Board of Overseers for the Baldrige Program at this pivotal point in its history.

Now, in 2011, U.S. competitiveness is again at risk, with a new set of Asian challengers from China and emerging market countries. The early 21st century adds some new performance pressures on companies. Environmental impact and social responsibility have been added to the agenda. The rise of the Internet makes customers more knowledgeable and less forgiving, given their access to information about numerous choices; after all, global companies can source from anywhere in the world. Transparency makes it harder for companies to hide mistakes. Some of their mistakes have enormously disastrous consequences, such as the BP oil spill in the Gulf of Mexico. The era of information-driven globalization is characterized by frequent, rapid and sometimes unpredictable change, both done by leaders and done to them by events in the external world. Globalization increases the speed of change, as more competitors from more places produce surprises. System effects send ripples that spread to more places faster—innovations in one place proving disruptive in others, problems in one economy triggering problems in others.

This context makes the Baldrige Performance Criteria more necessary and appropriate than ever. Continuous improvement is not merely a good thing for a handful of companies but a survival strategy for every organization, as the only way to create organizations capable of rapid adjustment to rising standards and changing conditions. Indeed, the Baldrige Program has itself evolved to add more variables that have become critical to effectiveness in an intensely competitive global information economy. There is a high premium for innovation, the faster the better, as well as the ability to continuously upgrade products and processes.

The data and stories in this timely book make a convincing case that use of the Baldrige Criteria can help organizations assess and improve their performance, becoming more sophisticated about how to align all of their processes to achieve desired results. That is important not only to the success of manufacturing and service enterprises but also sectors such as health care and education which are vital to the future of the economy and the well-being of society. The Baldrige Award is given to only a few of the applicants because they meet the highest standards. But in a sense, every organization that uses the Baldrige Criteria for self-study and change can turn out to be a winner due to their increased ability to learn, adapt, innovate, and achieve excellence.

Rosabeth Moss Kanter is the Ernest L. Arbuckle Professor of Business Administration at Harvard Business School and chair and director of the Harvard University Advanced Leadership Initiative. She is author or coauthor of 18 books. Her latest book is SuperCorp: How Vanguard Companies Create Innovation, Profits, Growth, and Social Good.

Foreword

by Gregory R. Page

Building a high-performance organization in a volatile world can at times seem fairly elusive for those who are leading large institutions. From the growth of technology and shifting customer expectations to the emergence of new markets and global competition, it is clear that what it takes to be successful today is different from what it took just a decade ago—and certainly different from what it was when the U.S. Congress passed the Malcolm Baldrige National Quality Improvement Act in 1987. The purpose of the Act and the awards program it spawned was to enhance U.S. competitiveness by encouraging organizations to focus on quality and performance excellence. It did this by establishing criteria for evaluating improvement efforts, identifying and recognizing role-model organizations, and disseminating and sharing best practices.

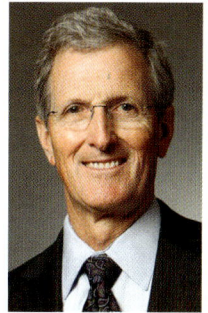

Baldrige 20/20: An Executive's Guide to the Criteria for Performance Excellence provides today's executives with practical examples and keen insights on how organizations can stay focused and excel. While the information shared here comes from Baldrige Award winners, this volume is neither a celebration of their accomplishments nor an arcane, overly complex view of every step taken in their journey. Instead, what you have here is a useful guide that substantively shares how others are successfully navigating the storms of change, achieving operational effectiveness and efficiency, improving financial results, enhancing customer service, and winning new markets through application of the Baldrige Criteria.

For those whose organizations have had the honor of receiving the Malcolm Baldrige National Quality Award, the real win comes not in a unit of a company or institution receiving the award but in what the efforts teach us about ourselves, our organizations, and what we can do to create a culture of performance excellence. At Cargill, our egg processing and corn milling businesses have both been recognized with Baldrige Awards. The businesses' collective efforts not only exposed improvements in operations, product quality, and food safety, but they have helped to fuel a business excellence ethic within the entire corporation where units in Asia, South America, Europe, and Africa, as well as North America, are now looking more closely at their processes and using Baldrige-type criteria to achieve continuous improvement and to give them an edge in the marketplace. In short, the Baldrige Criteria and methodology have been critical in helping us align our business strategy, engage our employees, and inspire our teams to constantly strive to improve every day.

At Cargill we are intent on building a balanced, diverse, and resilient organization. We aspire to be "the global leader in nourishing people." None of that is possible without trust—trust between ourselves and our customers, trust between ourselves and other stakeholders, trust that we will adhere to ethical standards, and trust that we will deliver quality products and do what we say we will do. Underlying that notion of trust is making sure one has the methods and processes in place to sustainably deliver against ever-increasing expectations and our desire for continuous improvement. The Baldrige Criteria and methodology have been foundational for us in that journey. *Baldrige 20/20* will shed light on how you and your organization might benefit from this as well.

Gregory R. Page is the chairman of the board and chief executive officer of Cargill, Incorporated. He joined Cargill in 1974 as a trainee and, over the years, has held a number of positions in the United States and overseas. He also serves as a member of the board of directors of Eaton Corporation and Carlson, and he is immediate past-chair of the board of Big Brothers Big Sisters of America.

Baldrige Performance Excellence Program

Dear Reader:

As an executive, you may ask the logical question, "Why should I read this book?" I have two answers for you: because you want your organization to survive and thrive as a respected organization today and a respected organization in the year 2020, and because 20/20 hindsight is easy but 20/20 foresight is not. Any leader can assess where he or she has been, as well as his or her successes and failures, but to establish the path for future success, track progress, and adjust course as needed are much more challenging. The Baldrige Award winners whose results, stories, and strategies are shared in this book provide guidance on achieving 20/20 foresight. They are competitiveness and innovation leaders, and they are worth emulating.

These are uncertain times for all enterprises. The future will be full of strategic challenges as we adjust to the shifting dimensions of our global economy. The Baldrige Criteria for Performance Excellence provide a framework for addressing these challenges and assessing progress. The organizations in this book are role models, and their success can be replicated, but *you* have to start the journey. This book will hopefully inspire you, through these role models' successes, to say, "I can face the future with confidence, strategy, and structure."

I have had the good fortune of being associated with the Baldrige Performance Excellence Program for almost 20 years. I have participated in the evolution of the Baldrige Criteria from a set of criteria for product quality to a set of criteria for organizational excellence. I have had the privilege of seeing organizations grow and change to meet new challenges and opportunities and to achieve role-model status. I have had the honor of meeting some of the most wonderful people, visionary leaders, and engaged employees our country has to offer. Through this book, I hope the courage, enthusiasm, and success of these people and their organizations will excite you to embark on your own Baldrige journey—your own journey to excellence and sustainability.

What led the organizations in this book to pursue a Baldrige journey? Some turned to Baldrige out of crisis. They were on the road to extinction and looking for a tool

Baldrige Performance Excellence Program ¦ National Institute of Standards and Technology | Department of Commerce
100 Bureau Drive, Stop 1020 ¦ Gaithersburg, MD 20899-1020 | (301) 975-2036 p ¦ (301) 948-3716 f ¦ baldrige@nist.gov ¦ www.nist.gov/baldrige

to save their organizations. They had heard about Baldrige and needed to do something very different from their current business model. In recent years, most organizations were doing well but were faced with an ever more complex environment. They were looking for a systems approach to achieve a sustainable competitive advantage.

As I write this introduction, I am on a flight from the fourth meeting of the Baldrige Executive Fellows to the Texas Award for Performance Excellence program's annual conference. The Executive Fellows came together almost a year ago for a year-long experience to learn from Baldrige Award winners by witnessing their performance firsthand at their sites and learning from their executives. Every session has been invigorating for them and me. The Texas program will showcase organizations on a Baldrige journey that have received recognition at the state level (70 percent of Baldrige Award winners start at their state or local Baldrige-based programs). This book will give you an introduction that documents why such companies, large and small; nonprofits; schools; and health care organizations, across the United States, are making this larger commitment to a Baldrige journey.

Are you still a skeptic about Baldrige? Are you willing to invest a few hours to look at the potential of Baldrige in your organization and then see if it is for you? Every journey begins with a single step. Take this first step, and then, I hope, you will challenge your organization to achieve excellence!

Many people and many organizations contributed to this book. I would like to thank two people on the Baldrige Program staff—Christine Schaefer and Dawn Bailey—who took the lead, believed in this project, and translated an idea into reality. I also would like to thank all the Baldrige Award winners who let us tell their stories. The family members of Secretary Malcolm Baldrige, for whom this program is named, have been strong supporters throughout the history of the program. And finally I would like to recognize Curt Reimann, the initial director of the program, who conceived what a business-government partnership could achieve and who wrote the first set of Baldrige Criteria in 1988.

Harry S. Hertz
Director, Baldrige Performance Excellence Program
Summer 2011

Baldrige Performance Excellence Program | National Institute of Standards and Technology | Department of Commerce
100 Bureau Drive, Stop 1020 | Gaithersburg, MD 20899-1020 | (301) 975-2036 p | (301) 948-3716 f | baldrige@nist.gov | www.nist.gov/baldrige

Introduction

Hindsight may be 20/20, but without a crystal ball, how can you make sound decisions now that will steer your organization toward success on the road ahead?

The Baldrige framework for performance excellence® is a validated management tool designed to help organizations do just that. The framework—the Criteria for Performance Excellence®—can help you improve your organization's current operations and achieve long-term sustainability. In fact, the 86 organizations that received the Baldrige Award between 1980 and 2010 have proven that applying the Baldrige Criteria to the way they run their businesses has led to better financial results; satisfied, loyal customers; improved products and services; and an engaged workforce.

While no management system can enable you to predict exactly what challenges will arise in the years—or days—to come, using the Baldrige Criteria as a framework for ongoing self-assessment and planning will mean that you are better prepared to meet even daunting, unexpected challenges. You will have a focus on results, and you will have systematic processes in place that are effective, fully deployed, agile, regularly evaluated for improvement, responsive to customer and stakeholder needs, and integrated into all operational areas. Your organization will also have the ability to innovate for the future.

The Criteria for Performance Excellence

The Criteria for Performance Excellence are a set of questions focusing on the critical aspects of management that help you guide your organization toward success and sustainability. Award-winning organizations use the Criteria for self-assessment, for improvement, and as a framework for performance excellence, integrating the Criteria into how they conduct business and/or care for patients or help students learn. Using the Criteria to assess your organization can help you align resources; improve communication, productivity, and effectiveness; and achieve strategic goals.

The Criteria are not prescriptive; they will not tell you what to do to gain results. Instead, they focus on the drivers of success and interrelated core values and concepts, from management by fact to visionary leadership, customer-driven excellence, and management for innovation. The preface of the Criteria, also called the Organizational Profile, consists of introductory sets of questions and is where you detail your company's strategic context, including challenges, advantages, and organizational relationships. Because the Organizational Profile sets a context for your organization, the Criteria can apply to every organization, large or small, across every sector of the U.S. economy.

The Sections of This Book

The next section, "**Representative Role Models and Data**," explains how role-model organizations have applied the Baldrige Criteria for Performance Excellence to how they run their businesses and received a huge return on their investments. Data are provided to show improvements in financial returns, customer and workforce satisfaction, and graduation rates, among many other measures. Data are presented by sector: manufacturing, service, small business, health care, education, and nonprofit. These data are compiled from publicly available sources in the years leading up to the organizations' receiving the Malcolm Baldrige National Quality Award.®

Baldrige Award winners' distinctive experiences in using the Criteria to attain performance excellence are detailed in "**Award Winners' Journeys: How Baldrige Led Them to Excellence**," complete with dos and don'ts to guide you if you decide to take the challenge.

In "**The Criteria: Framework for Performance Excellence**," you'll learn about the critical questions asked within the seven interrelated areas covered by this leading-edge management tool. Data are presented here on ethics and sustainability.

"**How Can the Baldrige Program Help You Now?**" details the steps you may want to take now as you begin your journey to performance excellence using the Criteria and the practices and guidance of Baldrige Award-winning organizations.

Finally, the appendix, "**Examples by Criteria Category**," provides a sampling of Baldrige Award winners' processes and results (current as of the year each won the award) to exemplify each of the seven Criteria categories.

Representative Role Models and Data

By adopting the systems perspective behind the Baldrige Criteria for Performance Excellence, executives of role-model organizations have improved their operations and results and even achieved breakthrough gains in performance. The organizations described in this section represent the best of the best in the U.S. manufacturing, service, small business, health care, education, and nonprofit sectors. All have received the Malcolm Baldrige National Quality Award, the highest level of recognition that a U.S. organization can receive for performance excellence, and all have used the feedback from their Baldrige assessments to build on their strengths and address their areas for improvement. As part of applying for the Baldrige Award, an applicant receives a feedback report from a team of trained examiners that outlines the organization's strengths and opportunities for improvement from the team's perspective.

The following pages contain some of these Baldrige Award winners' stories and the data that make the case for beginning *your* organization's Baldrige quest toward excellence.

The Case for Baldrige:
Model of Excellence in Manufacturing

"The economic environment is difficult for Cargill Corn Milling, as it is difficult for many manufacturing companies today. But . . . by utilizing the processes and tools that we've learned from Baldrige, we're able to not only meet these challenges but actually excel in them."

Alan Willits, President and Business Unit Leader
Cargill Corn Milling
2008 Baldrige Award winner

Cargill Corn Milling North America (CCM), based in Wayzata, Minnesota, is a business unit within privately held Cargill, Inc., that manufactures corn- and sugar-based products. CCM has a workforce of 2,321 employees and delivers 60-plus products to more than 3,000 customers in food, feed, and fermentation markets.

With revenues of more than $1 billion a year, CCM saw its earnings after taxes nearly triple in the four years preceding its recognition as a Baldrige Award winner in 2008. In addition, its cost of doing business—expense as a percentage of gross profit—decreased from about 35 percent to 30 percent over three years. In this measure, Cargill exceeded competitive benchmarks by at least 5 percent over that period.

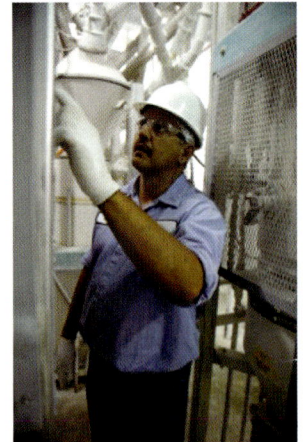

CCM has been using the Baldrige Criteria as a self-assessment framework since the early 1990s (see the story of its performance excellence journey on page 56). Today, the company's focus on continuous improvement is evident in its ongoing efforts to increase operational reliability and effectiveness through such approaches as real-time and predictive monitoring of equipment health, stringent maintenance, and careful energy usage. As a result, CCM maintained steady per-bushel costs from fiscal year (FY) 2006 to FY2008 even though energy, chemical, and maintenance costs increased 50 to 80 percent, 30 percent, and 10 percent, respectively.

"Good processes do not insulate us from reality, but they do give us the structure to recover in tough times and improve in good times," Willits stated at the Baldrige Program's annual Quest for Excellence® conference in 2009. "Food safety is a critical element of our manufacturing and delivery processes. We make ingredients that go into many major food products. For example, one railcar of high fructose can sweeten approximately 2 million cans of soft drinks. In some cases, our product will be on the grocery store shelves within 36 hours of production. This requires rigid food safety standards and controls to protect all consumers, including employees and their families."

Food Safety Scores

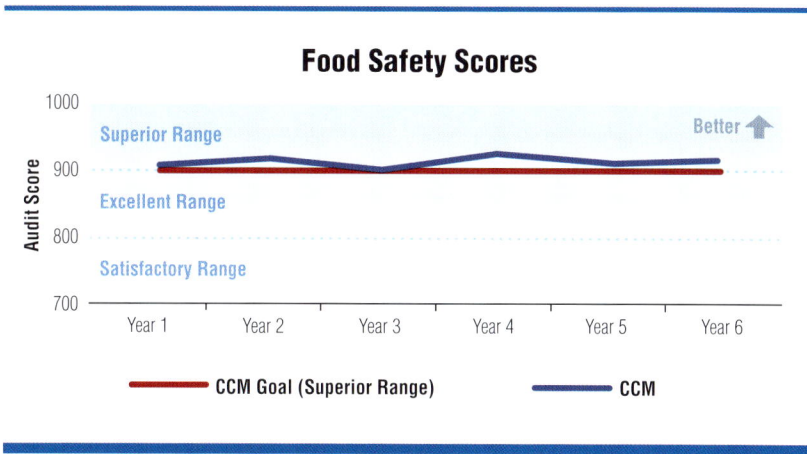

As the chart shows, CCM's facilities have maintained scores in the superior range during third-party audits. Yet, said Willits, "No matter how well we score, we can never compromise our standards."

The Proof Is in the Data, Part 1:
The Baldrige Effect on Manufacturing

Since 2000, ten manufacturing organizations have received the Baldrige Award:

- a subunit of a large independent manufacturer that designs, produces, and assembles driveshafts and related components and provides related services
- a contract manufacturer of precision sheet metal and machined components for the telecommunications, semiconductor, and medical equipment industries
- a printer and supplier of check products and related services to financial institutions
- a business unit that produces commercial and industrial radio products, as well as communications and information technology
- a company with a large market share in developing, manufacturing, marketing, and servicing medical devices used to diagnose and treat disease
- a privately held corporation that manufactures frozen, ready-to-use food products
- a manufacturer of egg-based food products that is a subsidiary of a large, privately held international corporation providing food and agricultural products
- a manufacturer of corn- and sugar-based food products that is a business unit of a large, privately held international corporation providing food and agricultural products
- a contractor that specializes in electrical, mechanical, and engineered material components for national defense systems
- a manufacturer of packaged dog and cat food

In the years leading up to recognition as Baldrige Award winners, these manufacturers achieved very favorable results that directly improved revenues, customer satisfaction, and employee satisfaction, as well as other performance measures. These achievements are highlighted below.

IMPROVED FINANCIAL RESULTS

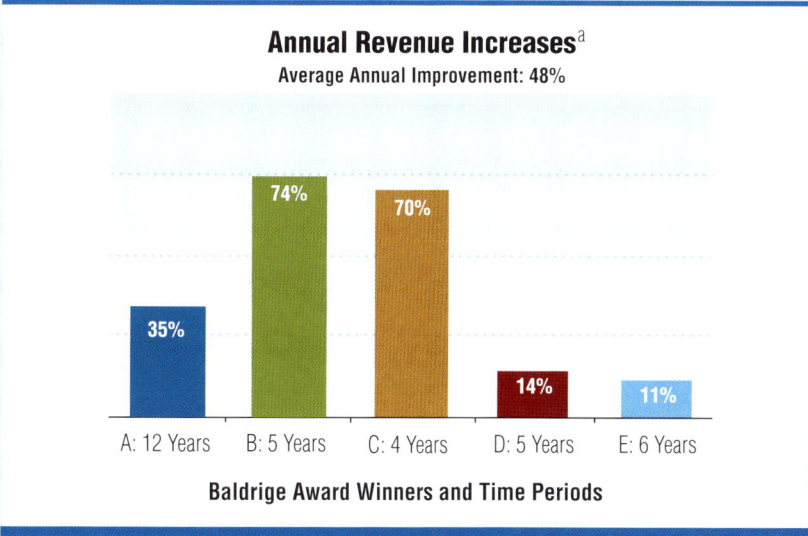

Annual Revenue Increases[a]
Average Annual Improvement: 48%

Baldrige Award Winners and Time Periods	
A: 12 Years	35%
B: 5 Years	74%
C: 4 Years	70%
D: 5 Years	14%
E: 6 Years	11%

[a] Five manufacturers did not publicly report a comparable measure. These average improvement rates were sustained annually over the specified time periods, which reflect the most recent results reported by the manufacturers in the year each received the Baldrige Award.

- **Global sales of $12.5 billion in the year it won the Baldrige Award**. In addition, the company increased its revenue over the 7 years leading up to its Baldrige Award despite marginal growth in the U.S. pet population during the same period. (Nestlé Purina PetCare Company)

- **15-fold annual improvements in cost savings from supply-chain efforts, from $2 million to $65 million** over 2 years (Honeywell Federal Manufacturing & Technologies [FM&T])

- **20% annual cost savings from energy conservation improvements** for 3 years (Honeywell FM&T)

- **$23.5 million to $27 million annual cost savings from deployed innovations and increased productivity** for 3 fiscal years (Honeywell FM&T)

- **More than $7.5 million annual cost savings from implementing innovative ideas** for 2 years (Cargill Corn Milling)

SATISFIED CUSTOMERS

Customer Satisfaction Levels[a]

A	B	C	D	E	F
95%	96%	100%	88%	96%	80%

Baldrige Award Winners

[a]Four manufacturers did not publicly report a comparable measure. The levels shown above reflect the last year reported before the award.

1. Manufacturer A reported customer satisfaction of 95% or higher for 4 years, compared with the commercial industry's best-in-class levels of 78% to 85%.

2. Manufacturer B reported 100% customer satisfaction rates for 4 years in 3 of 5 key indicators (on-time delivery, technical support, and customer service access) and rates above 90% for its other 2 key indicators (product performance and product freshness).

3. Manufacturer C's customer satisfaction rate increased 11% annually for 3 years.

4. In addition to overall customer satisfaction and repurchase/recommend rates exceeding 88% for 4 years, 99% of Manufacturer D's customers were "satisfied" or "very satisfied" with customer service in the last year reported.

5. In surveys of partner organizations, Manufacturer E sustained a 96% satisfaction rate for 5 years.

6. Manufacturer F's overall customer satisfaction levels averaged more than 80% for 3 years, a performance that was better than that of all its competitors.

- **99.9% combined quality/reliability ratings** by traditional customers and **98.4% to 99% ratings** by nontraditional customers for 3 years (Honeywell FM&T)

- **96% customer loyalty**—customers willing to continue working with the company—over 4 quarters, beating the commercial industry's best-in-class level of 95% for same period (Honeywell FM&T)

- **23% annual decline in customer incidents**—complaints and rejections per 1,000 shipments—from 10.5 to 3.3 over 3 years (Cargill Corn Milling)

- **Nearly 12% annual decline in customer complaints per shipment** in 3 years. The company improved these results despite an increase in shipments of 18% over 5 years. (Cargill Corn Milling)

- **From 1996 to 2003, improvement from the top 20 to 2nd** in a ranking of customer satisfaction among more than 50 medical imaging companies. In addition, from 2001 to 2010, this company's global customer satisfaction ratings using the Net Promoter scoring system, which measures customer loyalty based on willingness to refer, have shown **steady improvement from 50% to 63%, surpassing the best-in-class benchmark of 50%.** (MEDRAD, Inc.)

A Satisfied, Stable Workforce

Workforce Satisfaction Levels[a]

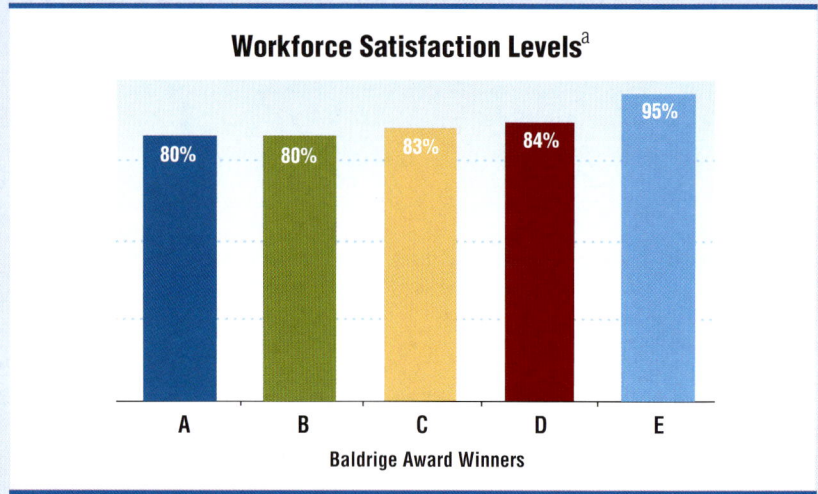

Bar chart showing Workforce Satisfaction Levels for Baldrige Award Winners:
- A: 80%
- B: 80%
- C: 83%
- D: 84%
- E: 95%

[a]Five manufacturers did not publicly report a comparable measure. The levels shown above reflect the last year reported before the award.

1. Manufacturer A's total score on its employee satisfaction survey improved 14% over 4.5 years, or 3% annually, and the company neared world-class levels on core employee satisfaction questions based on an industry benchmark provided by the Hogan Center for Performance Excellence.

2. For Manufacturer B, after overall employee satisfaction equaled or outperformed that of the top 20 companies in Hay Group employee surveys for at least 4 consecutive years, the company switched to a new benchmark in order to promote continuous improvement. Over the next 2 years, its overall employee satisfaction rate improved by approximately 10 percentage points, approaching the best-in-class standard of 90%.

3. Overall employee satisfaction scores for Manufacturer C were higher than those of its competitors. The company sustained excellent levels for 5 consecutive years.

4. Manufacturer D achieved a 3% annual improvement rate over 6 years, with the most current results outperforming those of two peers identified as benchmarks by this manufacturer.

5. Manufacturer E's results on an employee job satisfaction measure improved by more than 10% over 3 years, and its results were the best in its city.

- **72% employee satisfaction scores on "feels appreciated" survey item**, compared to the commercial (private) industry's best-in-class level of 67%; **81% employee satisfaction scores on "management listens to ideas,"** compared to the commercial industry's best-in-class level of 76%; **72% employee satisfaction scores on "positive environment,"** compared to the commercial industry's best-in-class level of 58%; **80% employee satisfaction scores on "information provided"** to employees, compared to the commercial industry's best-in-class level of 65% (Honeywell FM&T)

- **19% annual improvement rate in overall employee engagement** on company survey for 4 years (Cargill Corn Milling)

- **8% employee turnover rate**, compared to 12% industry average reported by the Bureau of National Affairs (Cargill Corn Milling)

- For 3 years, **8% annual decrease in workforce turnover**, which was previously as high as 30% annually (Sunny Fresh Foods [now Cargill Kitchen Solutions])

- **4% annual improvement in workforce turnover** for 5 years, better than a benchmark based on data from *Fortune* magazine's "Top 10 Places to Work" in 5 of 6 years (MEDRAD, Inc.)

Improved Operations

- **95% operational reliability effectiveness rate**—a ratio between actual production and commercial demand—3 percentage points shy of the world-class benchmark set by the Society of Maintenance and Reliability Professionals (Cargill Corn Milling)

- Over 5 years, **42% improvement in operational asset health**, which increased from 60% healthy assets to 85%, the world-class level (Cargill Corn Milling)

The Case for Baldrige:
A Service Company's Success Story

"Today, 1,700 not-for-profit hospitals—and the patients they serve—are the beneficiaries of [a vision born from the Baldrige Criteria]. . . . Together we have achieved billions of dollars in savings—savings that strengthen the ability of hospitals to provide quality care."

Richard A. Norling, President/CEO
Premier Inc.
2006 Baldrige Award winner

Premier Inc. is the largest health care alliance in the United States, serving approximately 1,700 hospitals and more than 43,000 other health care sites, including nursing homes and ambulatory care centers. More than 900 employees serve at the health care alliance's headquarters in Charlotte, North Carolina, and in offices in San Diego, California, and Washington, D.C. To improve patient outcomes while safely reducing the cost of care, the Premier health care alliance's three business units provide members with group purchasing and supply-chain management, insurance and risk management, and informatics and performance improvement tools. Formed in 1996 from three smaller alliances, the company is now owned by some 200 nonprofit health care providers and health system organizations. The strategic alliance enables the owners to share services and programs aimed at improving the quality and cost-effectiveness of clinical operations.

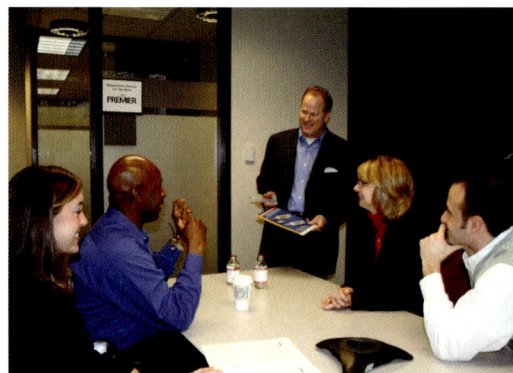

From the start, Premier Inc.'s executives set a goal for its member hospitals to deliver the best, most cost-effective care in the nation and for the health care alliance to have a major influence on reshaping health care. To that end, the alliance has focused its business units on driving measurable improvement and performance breakthroughs in disciplines where such opportunities exist. The success of this strategy is evident in the company's financial results. Savings and cash returns to its hospital owners increased from approximately $180 million to $804 million over four years. During that period, the company's total revenue rose from approximately $410 million to over $500 million. Premier Inc. also increased its consolidated pretax operating income from approximately $140 million to approximately $223 million, which exceeded or equaled that of its largest single competitor in each of those years. While Premier Inc.'s operating margin increased from 35 percent to 50 percent over three years and was higher than the top competitor's in each year, its operating expenses remained well below the competitor's.

In addition to achieving impressive financial results, the Premier health care alliance has been a leader in establishing and promoting best practices and methods for driving ethical conduct, transparency, and accountability within the group purchasing community. For example, Premier Inc. created the Healthcare Group Purchasing Industry Initiative to promote and monitor best ethical practices in purchasing for hospitals and other health care providers. As a result of its efforts, all the major health care organizations involved in cooperative purchasing have committed to publicly reporting key information.

At the 2007 Quest for Excellence conference, Premier Inc. President and CEO Richard A. Norling characterized the Baldrige Criteria as useful to the uniquely structured organization from its start. "We had the great opportunity [in 1996] to create a new-generation health care alliance, going well beyond the shared services organization," Norling said. At the same time, added Norling, his company faced great challenges at the outset—"the challenges you might expect in newly merging organizations in a changing health care and business environment."

Yet, like other organizations, the Premier health care alliance reportedly found the Criteria for Performance Excellence helpful in achieving success and applicable to its unique situation. "Embedding Baldrige was crucial to our shaping Premier successfully from these beginnings," said Norling. "It is very true that the Criteria, not being prescriptive, apply to all kinds of organizations in all kinds of situations."

The Proof Is in the Data, Part 2:
The Baldrige Effect on Service

Since 2000, five service organizations have received the Baldrige Award:

- an operations and maintenance contractor for small to midsized wastewater and water-treatment systems
- a business unit that provides maintenance, modification, repair, and training for aircraft crews and maintenance staff
- the financial services business unit of a manufacturer of construction and mining equipment, gas and diesel engines, and industrial turbines
- the contractor that operates and maintains the U.S. Strategic Petroleum Reserve
- the largest U.S. health care alliance

In the years leading up to recognition as Baldrige Award winners, these organizations achieved favorable results that directly improved revenues, market share, and customer satisfaction, as well as other measures. These achievements are highlighted below.

IMPROVED FINANCIAL RESULTS

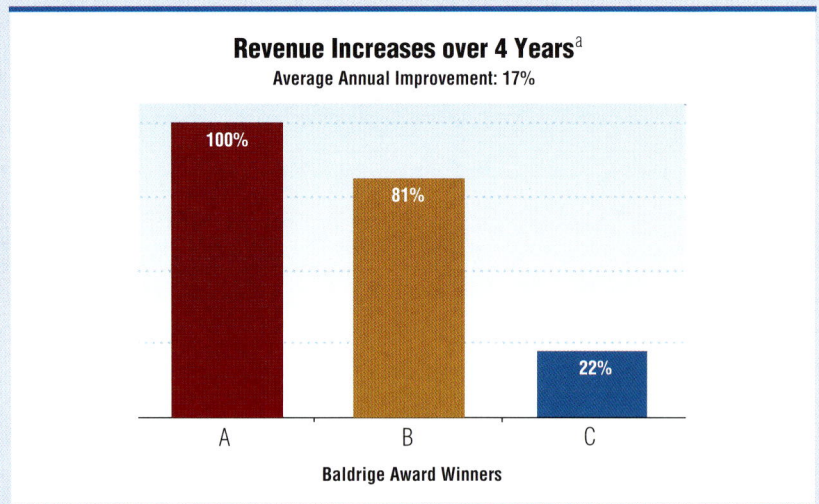

Revenue Increases over 4 Years[a]
Average Annual Improvement: 17%

A: 100%	B: 81%	C: 22%

Baldrige Award Winners

[a]Two businesses in the service sector did not publicly report a comparable measure. These results reflect the most recent time periods reported in the year each business received the Baldrige Award.

1. Service Business A realized this growth in a flat market, resulting in a loss of market share for its competitors.

2. For Service Business B, total revenue grew at an average annual rate of 15% over this period while its top competitor's revenue grew less than 5% annually.

Baldrige 20/20: An Executive's Guide to the Criteria for Performance Excellence

3. In addition to this increase in revenue, Service Business C's consolidated pretax operating income increased at an average annual rate of nearly 15%.

- **Nearly 7% per year increase in market share** on average in the core business segment over 3 years (Operations Management International, Inc. [now CH2M HILL])

- **34% increase in assets and 54% increase in profit** over 5 years, against industry declines of 21% and 35%, respectively (Caterpillar Financial Services Corporation-U.S.)

- **Customer award fees about 70% higher than earned by the previous contractor** over 5 years (DynMcDermott Petroleum Operations Company [now DM Petroleum Operations Company])

- **Nearly 20% average annual increase in consolidated pretax operating income** over 4 years (Premier Inc.)

SATISFIED CUSTOMERS

Customer Satisfaction Levels[a]

A	B	C	D	E
75%	93%	94%	78%	89%

Baldrige Award Winners

[a]The levels shown above reflect the last year reported before the award.

1. Service Business A's customer satisfaction level exceeded the best-practice threshold of 60% for the survey.

2. Customer satisfaction in Service Business B's largest division was world-class in the industry and the American Customer Satisfaction Index.

3. Service Business C's customer satisfaction level reflects a 27% increase over 6 years.

4. Service Business D's customer satisfaction level was 6 percentage points higher than that of its best competitor.

5. Service Business E's customer satisfaction level reflects a 13% increase over 3 years.

- **95% of contracts renewed by its customers** in the year the Baldrige Award was received (Operations Management International [now CH2M HILL])

- **Highest average length of customer retention in the industry** in the year the Baldrige Award was received (Operations Management International [now CH2M HILL])

- **95% customer loyalty and 97% customer retention** in the year the Baldrige Award was received (Premier Inc.)

A Stable, Satisfied Workforce

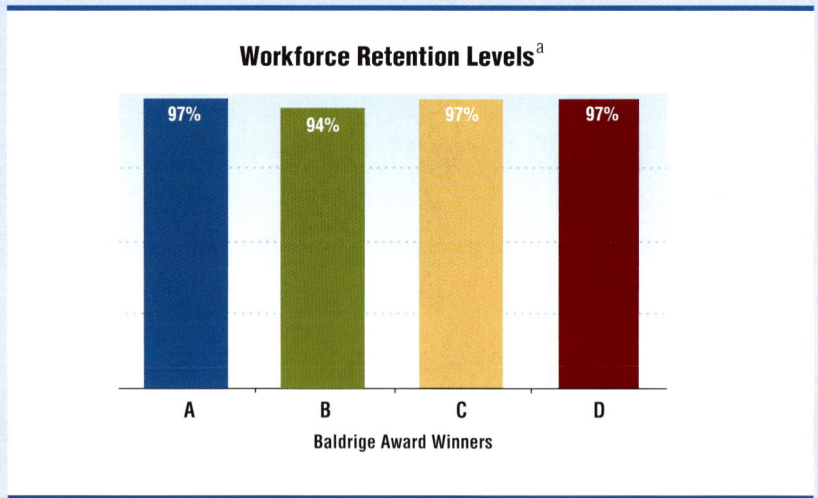

Workforce Retention Levels[a]

A	B	C	D
97%	94%	97%	97%

Baldrige Award Winners

[a]One business in the service sector did not publicly report a comparable measure. The levels shown above reflect the last year reported before the award.

- **39% decrease in employee turnover** over 5 years, to 16%, against an industry average of just over 27% (Operations Management International [now CH2M HILL])

- **80% of employees recommending the company** as a good place to work against a national norm of 55% in the year the Baldrige Award was received (Caterpillar Financial Services Corporation-U.S.)

- **Employee satisfaction 50 percentage points higher than the industry benchmark** set by Business Research Laboratory in the year the Baldrige Award was received (DynMcDermott Petroleum Operations Company [now DM Petroleum Operations Company])

Excellent Service

- **22% average drop in industrial customers' operating costs** over 2 years (Operations Management International [now CH2M HILL])

- **Improvement from 95% to 99% in drawdown readiness** for the U.S. Strategic Petroleum Reserve over 6 years; the company's service performance also has distinguished it as the global benchmark for cost-efficiency in crude oil storage systems (DynMcDermott Petroleum Operations Company [now DM Petroleum Operations Company])

- **More than $2.5 billion in savings for partner hospitals** through cooperative purchasing and other services offered by the organization over 3 years (Premier Inc.)

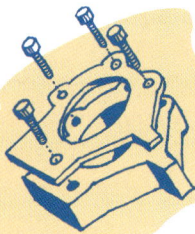

The Case for Baldrige:
Benefits for a Small Business

"The Baldrige Award application process has provided our company with many learning and continuous improvement opportunities, making PRO-TEC better for the endeavor."

W. Paul Worstell, President (1997–2010)
PRO-TEC Coating Company
2007 Baldrige Award winner

Established in 1990 as a joint venture between United States Steel Corporation and Kobe Steel Ltd. of Japan, **PRO-TEC Coating Company** provides coated sheet steel primarily to the U.S. automotive industry for use in manufacturing cars, trucks, and sport utility vehicles. PRO-TEC's 236 employees, called "Associates," work in a state-of-the-art, 730,000-square-foot facility surrounded by corn and soybean fields in the small, rural town of Leipsic, Ohio. When it received the Baldrige Award, PRO-TEC had been profitable for more than a decade; sales reached $846 million in 2006.

Systems reliability is critical to PRO-TEC. The company has developed a stringent preventive maintenance program that includes routine scheduled outages and critical spare parts stored on-site. In the four years before it received the Baldrige Award, PRO-TEC had led the industry by operating 98 percent of the time. Over that period, PRO-TEC produced no less than 85 percent of the United States' advanced high-strength steel supply. Revenue per Associate reached approximately $4 million, nearly four times the *Industry Week* 90th percentile benchmark, demonstrating PRO-TEC's industry leadership in this area. In a capital-intensive industry, PRO-TEC's return on assets, a measure of long-term viability, sustained an upward trend for four years beginning in 2002. PRO-TEC consistently fulfilled its customers' expectations of quality by delivering products with a defect rate of less than 0.12 percent. In a 2005 and 2006 survey of customers—covering product quality, on-time delivery, service, product development, and overall performance—PRO-TEC scored better than its competition in all categories.

PRO-TEC is a role model for its focus on its workforce. As the figure below shows, in the two-year period before it received the Baldrige Award, PRO-TEC maintained a recordable injury frequency of fewer

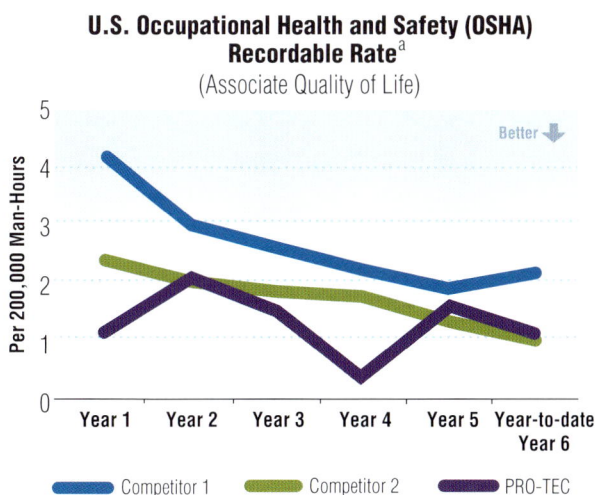

U.S. Occupational Health and Safety (OSHA) Recordable Rate[a]
(Associate Quality of Life)

[a]The OSHA Recordable Rate is an employee injury and illness incidence measure used to evaluate organizational safety.

Turnover Rate
(Associate Quality of Life)

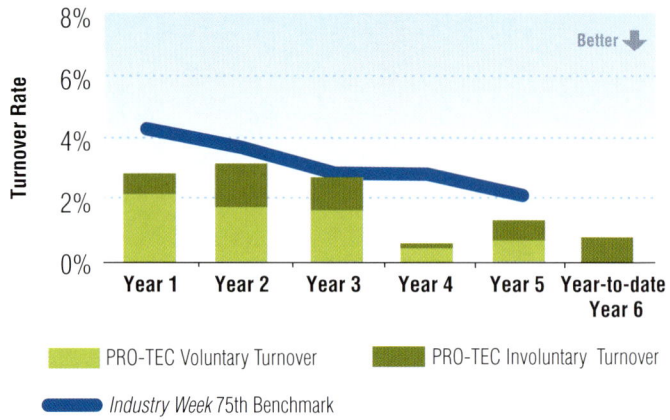

than two injuries per 200,000 man-hours—lower than the industry benchmark. Turnover rate (shown in the figure above), another key indicator of PRO-TEC Associates' quality of life, was less than 3 percent—consistently better than *Industry Week*'s "Best Plants" 75th-percentile level. As of the year it received the Baldrige Award, PRO-TEC had never laid off an Associate.

The Proof Is in the Data, Part 3:
The Baldrige Effect on Small Business

Since 2000, 12 small businesses, each with 500 or fewer employees, have received the Baldrige Award:

- an independent community bank
- a quick-service restaurant
- a printing, design, and mailing business
- a chemical-specialty manufacturing and sales company
- a screen-printing, photo-engraving, and chemical-etching business
- a luxury car dealership
- a service business providing corrosion protection systems
- a joint venture that provides coated sheet steel
- a family-owned catalog and Internet retailer offering shooting, reloading, gunsmithing, and hunting products
- a consulting firm offering engineering, architecture, environmental science, planning, program management, and construction services
- a management company that has created two fast-casual restaurant concepts and implemented these at seven locations
- a health care consulting firm

Following are some favorable Baldrige effects for these small businesses—highlighted improvements or high levels achieved on key measures over the three years or more leading up to each organization's role-model recognition.

Increasing Sales, Profits, and Market Share

- **More than 40% annual gross profit,** exceeding the industry standard (K&N Management)

- **More than 30% annual growth in revenues** for the past 9 years, exceeding the Association of Management Consulting Firms average of 10% annual growth (Studer Group)

- **Annual revenue growth of 12% to 16%** for the past 4 years, despite minimal growth in the engineering industry (Freese and Nichols Inc.)

- **93% increase in sales** over 6 years (MESA Products, Inc.)

- **25% sales growth rate** in 1 year, compared to 10% for its competitor; **300% increase in net income as a percentage of sales** over 5 years (MidwayUSA)

- **51% increase in gross profit percentage** over 4 years and **30% increase in new and preowned cars sold** over 4 years; **11% growth in share** of luxury car market at the Plano dealership over 3 years (Park Place Lexus)

- **11% increase in profitability** over 6 years (Texas Nameplate Company, Inc.)

- **48% growth in net income** over 4 years; **5% growth in share of primary customers** over 2 years (Los Alamos National Bank)

- **172% improvement in market share** in its primary service area over 4 years; **72% growth in sales** over 4 years, a gain held in 2002, when the industry declined 6.6% (Branch-Smith Printing Division)

- **400% increase in sales** over 12 years (Stoner)

- **Almost doubling of market share** over 7 years (Pal's Sudden Service)

INCREASING CUSTOMER SATISFACTION AND RETENTION

Customer Satisfaction Levels[a]

A: 93% · B: 87% · C: 98% · D: 87% · E: 96% · F: 84% · G: 92% · H: 99%

Baldrige Award Winners

[a]Four small businesses did not publicly report a comparable measure. The levels shown above reflect the last year reported before the award.

1. Customer satisfaction for Small Business A was greater than 90% for 3 years.

2. Small Business B realized a 7% gain in customer satisfaction over 3 years.

3. Customer satisfaction for Small Business C was 94% or higher for 5 years. Small Business C's customer satisfaction level represents a 2% gain over 4 years.

4. For Small Business D, customer satisfaction increased 4% over 6 years.

5. For Small Business E, customer satisfaction increased 5% over 6 years.

6. Customer satisfaction with Small Business F exceeded the national average and was higher than satisfaction with all other area institutions offering the same service.

7. Small Business G's result above reflects the average of responses to the 9 questions on the company's client survey. This business realized a nearly 40% increase over 3 years in survey ratings of its staff by satisfied clients.

8. Small Business H's 99% exceeded its best competitor's average rating of 85%.

Customer Retention Levels[a]

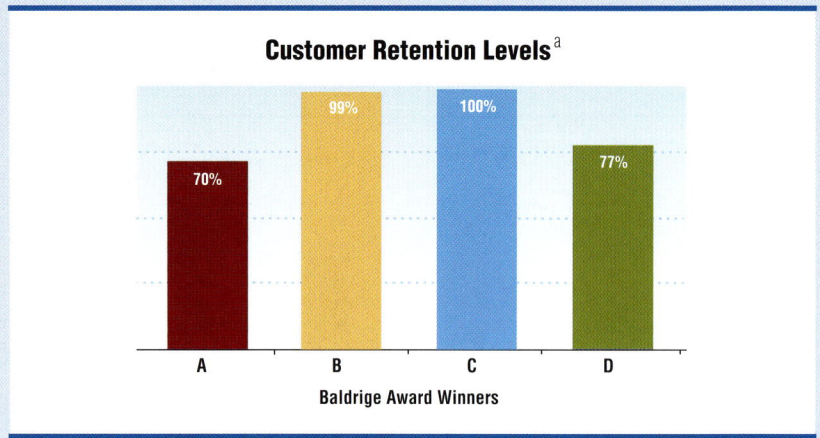

Baldrige Award Winners

A: 70%
B: 99%
C: 100%
D: 77%

[a]Eight small businesses did not publicly report a comparable measure. The levels shown above reflect the last year reported before the award.

1. Small Business A sustained a 70% retention rate for its top 50 customers for more than 10 years.

2. Over 5 years, Small Business B retained an average of 98% of its top customers, who accounted for over 60% of its business.

3. Small Business C improved customer retention 16% over 6 years.

4. Small Business D improved customer retention 14% over 4 years.

Improving Employee Measures

- **37% improvement in employee satisfaction** over 6 years (Stoner)

- **28% improvement in employee satisfaction** over 5 years and **12% increase in training hours per employee** over 2 years (Branch-Smith Printing Division)

- **37% decrease in turnover rate** over 5 years; its turnover rate in the year before it received the Baldrige Award was 127% when its best competitor's turnover rate topped 300% (Pal's Sudden Service)

- **11% improvement in employee satisfaction** over 2 years; more than **80% of the workforce cross-trained** to perform multiple tasks across departments (Texas Nameplate Company, Inc.)

- **1,533% improvement in the average training hours per employee** over 4 years; **48% improvement in turnover relative to satisfaction** over 8 years (Park Place Lexus)

- **38% decrease in employee turnover** over 5 years and **50% improvement in attendance at training** over 2 years (Los Alamos National Bank)

- **78% improvement in training investment in dollars** over 4 years (MESA Products, Inc.)

- **37% improvement in employee satisfaction and engagement** over 6 years (MidwayUSA)

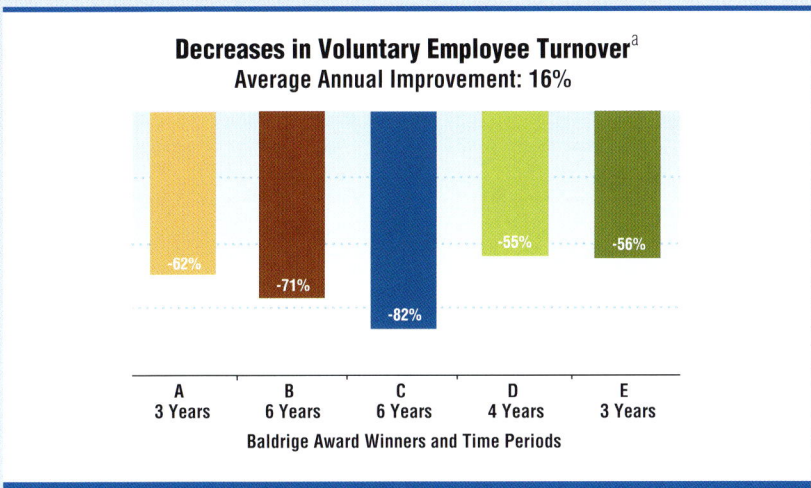

Decreases in Voluntary Employee Turnover[a]
Average Annual Improvement: 16%

A 3 Years	B 6 Years	C 6 Years	D 4 Years	E 3 Years
-62%	-71%	-82%	-55%	-56%

Baldrige Award Winners and Time Periods

[a] Seven small businesses did not publicly report a comparable measure. These results reflect the most recent time periods reported by the small businesses in the year each received the Baldrige Award.

Reducing Defects and Nonconformances

- **33% improvement in price of nonconformances as percentage of sales** over 6 years (Branch-Smith Printing Division)

- **54% decrease in warehouse errors/orders billed** over 5 years (Stoner)

- **40% improvement in product return rate** over 6 years (MidwayUSA)

- **64% improvement in product nonconformity with specifications,** as a percentage of sales over 6 years (Texas Nameplate Company, Inc.)

Ensuring On-Time Delivery

- **97% on-time shipping**, which represents a 4% improvement over 5 years (MESA Products, Inc.)

- **98% same-day shipping**, which represents a 1% improvement over 7 years while improving the cut-off time for guaranteed same-day shipping from 2 p.m. to 6 p.m. (MidwayUSA)

- **100% orders shipped same day**, which represents an 8% improvement over 4 years (Stoner)

- **98% on-time delivery**, which represents a 3% improvement over 3 years (Branch-Smith Printing Division)

Increasing Productivity and Return on Assets

- **30% increase in order handout speed** over 6 years; sales per labor hour improved by about $6 over 3 years (Pal's Sudden Service)

- **17% improvement in productivity** as measured by revenue per employee over 7 years (MESA Products, Inc.)

- **150% improvement in manufacturing productivity** over 12 years; **33% increase in weekly average output** of aerosol can products over 5 years; **39% return on assets** exceeds the industry average by 29% and the best competitor by 14% (Stoner)

The Case for Baldrige:
A Health Care Role Model

"As soon as you become a Baldrige organization, it will cost you less to run your business, and your outcomes will be better."

Rulon Stacey, President
Poudre Valley Health System
2008 Baldrige Award winner

Poudre Valley Health System (PVHS) is a private, nonprofit health care organization based in Fort Collins, Colorado. With a current workforce of 5,300, the organization provides a full spectrum of health care services to residents of northern Colorado, western Nebraska, and southern Wyoming through two hospitals (Poudre Valley Hospital in Fort Collins and the Medical Center of the Rockies in Loveland, Colorado) and a network of clinics and other care facilities.

PVHS stands out as a role model in its sector. It ranked in the national top 10% of similar organizations for low mortality and high satisfaction among patients, in the top 3% for employee satisfaction, and in the top 1% for physician loyalty. For each of the five years leading up to its Baldrige Award, Thomson Reuters named PVHS a "Top 100 Hospital," and *Modern Healthcare* named PVHS one of the "Top 100 Best Places to Work." Its excellence in nursing was recognized by designation as a Magnet hospital by the American Nurses Credentialing Center, and the National Database of Nursing Quality Indicators honored PVHS with the Outstanding Nursing Quality Award. PVHS also remained competitively priced in its regional health care market, generating $1 billion in annual revenue.

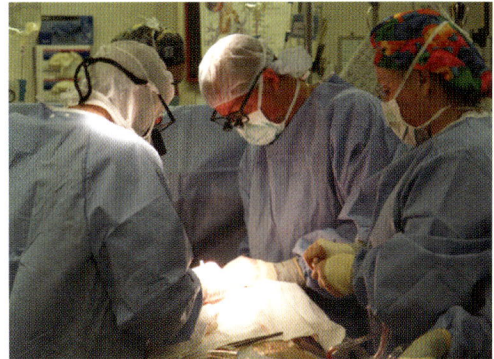

"Our patients and community told us they want high-quality, low-cost care. The Malcolm Baldrige National Quality Award demonstrates that we are giving our customers what they asked for and that we can do so for years to come," said Stacey. "Through the Baldrige process, we've learned that we need to learn. That's one of the best parts about Baldrige."

In the years preceding its Baldrige Award, PVHS consistently maintained competitive health care costs relative to local competitors with a similar patient base and to average costs in the Denver metropolitan area, which is PVHS's secondary service area. In 2006, the average PVHS charge was $2,000 lower than that of its main competitor and $7,000 lower than the average charge in the Denver metropolitan area. While committed to being a low-cost provider and despite declining reimbursements, Poudre Valley Hospital dramatically increased its profit per discharge to a level greater than that of the top 10 percent of U.S. hospitals, as the figure below shows. These results help PVHS achieve its mission of remaining an independent, nonprofit organization.

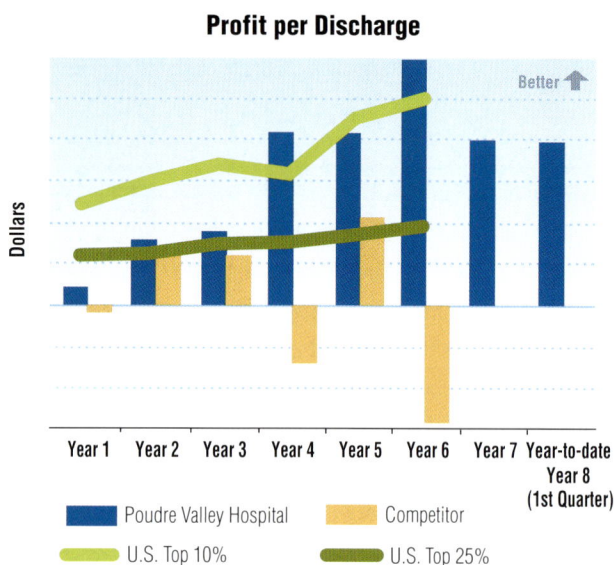

Profit per Discharge

Baldrige 20/20: An Executive's Guide to the Criteria for Performance Excellence

The Proof Is in the Data, Part 4:
The Baldrige Effect on Health Care

Since 2002, when the first organization received the Baldrige Award in the health care category, 12 organizations have been so honored:

- a private health care system that operates 17 acute care hospitals in Missouri, Illinois, Wisconsin, and Oklahoma
- the largest hospital in the Kansas City, Missouri, metropolitan area
- the largest health care system in the Florida Panhandle
- a private, nonprofit acute care hospital in New Jersey that includes environments to promote healing through art and nature
- an all-private-room facility located on a 28-acre urban campus in Michigan
- the largest rural, nonprofit hospital in the United States
- an integrated health care system in Wisconsin and Illinois
- San Diego County's largest integrated health care delivery system
- a locally owned health care organization serving residents of Colorado, Nebraska, and Wyoming
- a nonprofit New Jersey health care system
- a community-based health system serving residents of Missouri, Kansas, Nebraska, and Iowa
- an acute-care medical facility in suburban Chicago that is part of one of the nation's top-ten health systems

In the years leading up to their recognition as Baldrige Award winners, these organizations achieved the beneficial results highlighted below.

Decreasing Mortality Rates

- **24% reduction over 3 years in risk-adjusted mortality rate** (overall mortality divided by expected mortality where 1 is the standard), exceeding the top-decile level for this hospital's six-county region as measured by Thomson Reuters (Advocate Good Samaritan Hospital)

- **25% reduction in overall mortality rate** over 5 years, a rate better than the state top quartile and equal to the Agency for Healthcare Research and Quality best comparisons (Robert Wood Johnson University Hospital Hamilton)

- **23% reduction in overall mortality rate** over 2 years (Heartland Health)

- **20% reduction in overall mortality rate** over 2 years, a rate within the CareScience (a risk-adjusted database) best-practice level that is defined as the top 15% of U.S. facilities (Bronson Methodist Hospital)

- **57% reduction in mortality resulting from pneumonia** over 3 years. The decreased mortality rate represents approximately 100 fewer pneumonia-related deaths. (North Mississippi Medical Center)

- **95% reduction in mortality resulting from acute myocardial infarction** and **nearly 61% reduction in mortality resulting from congestive heart failure** over 4 years. The reduced rate was better than the Quadramed (a national organization providing comparative statistics for clinical operations) expected rate. (Robert Wood Johnson University Hospital Hamilton)

- **38% reduction in mortality resulting from congestive heart failure** over 4 years (Mercy Health System)

- **33% reduction in mortality resulting from congestive heart failure** over 4 years. The reduced rate was better than the Premier health care alliance's predicted rate. (AtlantiCare)

Rising Revenue and Market Share

- **24% increase in net operating margin** over 2 years, exceeding that of "AA"-rated hospitals. The operating margin level represents top-decile (in the upper 10%) performance in the industry. (Advocate Good Samaritan Hospital)

- **Nearly 71% increase in net revenue** over 5 years and a stable Moody's "A2" bond rating over 11 years (Mercy Health System)

- **11% compound annual growth rate in system revenues** for 9 years. This represents a 133% overall improvement or nearly 17% annual improvement rate. (AtlantiCare)

- **Top 10% of U.S. hospitals for total margin and operating margin** in 2009 and maintained Moody's and Fitch bond ratings of "A" and "A2" for 4 years (Heartland Health)

- **17% increase in overall market share** for its primary service area over 5 years (Bronson Methodist Hospital)

- **Market leadership position with 30% market share for cardiology, surgery, and oncology** (Robert Wood Johnson University Hospital Hamilton)

- **65% increase in total revenue** over 4 years. At the time it received the Baldrige Award, the organization outperformed the Council of Teaching Hospitals' top quartile in financial performance and ranked in the top 5% nationally in total margin. (Saint Luke's Hospital of Kansas City)

- **56% increase in net revenue** over 5 years. This represents an average annual growth rate of more than 11%. (Sharp HealthCare)

PATIENTS MORE SATISFIED

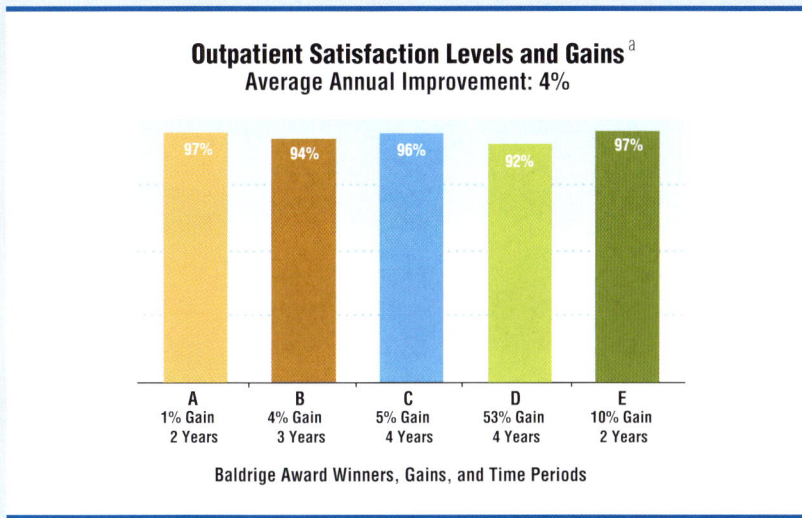

Outpatient Satisfaction Levels and Gains [a]
Average Annual Improvement: 4%

97%	94%	96%	92%	97%
A	**B**	**C**	**D**	**E**
1% Gain	4% Gain	5% Gain	53% Gain	10% Gain
2 Years	3 Years	4 Years	4 Years	2 Years

Baldrige Award Winners, Gains, and Time Periods

[a]Seven organizations in the health care sector did not publicly report a comparable measure. The levels shown above reflect the last year reported before the award.

Inpatient Satisfaction Levels and Gains[a]
Average Annual Improvement: 3%

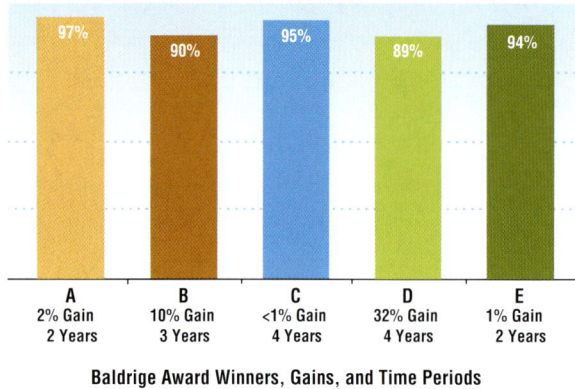

A	B	C	D	E
97%	90%	95%	89%	94%
2% Gain	10% Gain	<1% Gain	32% Gain	1% Gain
2 Years	3 Years	4 Years	4 Years	2 Years

Baldrige Award Winners, Gains, and Time Periods

[a]Seven organizations in the health care sector did not publicly report a comparable measure. The levels shown above reflect the last year reported before the award.

- **Ranking as "the nation's no. 1 hospital for overall patient satisfaction"** by Avatar (a patient satisfaction survey measurement tool administered by an independent third party) in the year before the organization as a whole received the Baldrige Award (Poudre Valley Health System's Medical Center of the Rockies). The **patient scores of the system's two hospitals surpass the national top 10%,** according to the Center for Medicare and Medicaid Services. (Poudre Valley Health System)

- **725% improvement in medical-group patient satisfaction with urgent care** and **100% improvement in overall medical-group patient satisfaction** over 5 years (Sharp HealthCare)

DECREASING EMPLOYEE TURNOVER AND VACANCY RATES

Decreases in Employee Turnover[a]

Average Annual Improvement: 15%

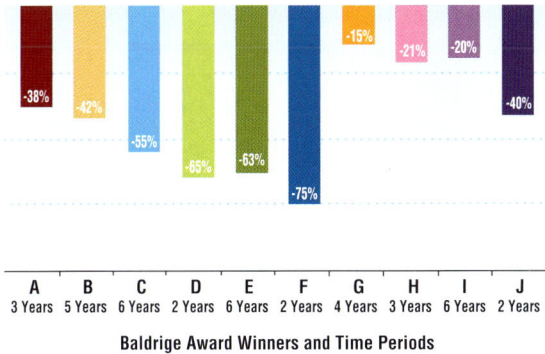

Baldrige Award Winners and Time Periods

[a]Two organizations in the health care sector did not publicly report a comparable measure. These results reflect the most recent time periods reported by the organizations in the year each received the Baldrige Award.

- **Decreases in employee vacancy rates: 68% decrease** over 3 years (Robert Wood Johnson University Hospital Hamilton); nearly **31% decrease** over 2 years (North Mississippi Medical Center); **34% decrease** over 5 years (Mercy Health System); **33% decrease** over 4 years (AtlantiCare)

- **Improvements in nurse vacancy, retention, or turnover rates:** nearly **50% decrease** over 2 years (Advocate Good Samaritan Hospital, registered nurse [RN] voluntary turnover rate); nearly **67% decrease** over 4 years (AtlantiCare, vacancy rate); nearly **28% decrease** over 3 years (Bronson Methodist Hospital, vacancy rate); **37% decrease** over 5 years (Mercy Health System, vacancy rate); **33% decrease** over 4 years (Poudre Valley Health System, vacancy rate); **67% increase** over 2 years (Robert Wood Johnson University Hospital, retention rate); **20% decrease** over 3 years (SSM Health Care, turnover rate)

Employees and Physicians More Satisfied

- **Nearly 19% improvement in employee satisfaction, to 4.75 out of 5** on a 5-point scale over 4 years (Bronson Methodist Hospital)

- **36% improvement in employee satisfaction** over 4 years. Satisfaction levels were equal to the Press Ganey benchmark in the year before the organization received the Baldrige Award. (Robert Wood Johnson University Hospital Hamilton)

- **11% improvement in employee satisfaction** over 4 years (Saint Luke's Hospital of Kansas City)

- **Nearly 47% improvement in physician satisfaction** over 3 years. In 2005, the satisfaction of physicians was 58%; in 2007, the focus was changed to quality of care as perceived by physicians, and the physician satisfaction level reached 85% in 2008. (AtlantiCare)

- **Nearly 20% improvement in physician satisfaction** over 2 years. Physicians rated the organization better than the Professional Research Consultants, Inc., norm for nursing care, responsiveness, discharge policy, and ease of scheduling. (Bronson Methodist Hospital)

- **99% overall physician satisfaction**—as well as satisfaction with ease of practice and leadership—as measured by Press Ganey, in the year the organization received the Baldrige Award (North Mississippi Medical Center)

- **National top 10% ranking,** according to Management Science Association (an independent national firm that conducts employee opinion surveys), **on 11 of 16 employee satisfaction areas,** including job satisfaction, senior management group, communications, pay, benefits, and performance management (Poudre Valley Health System)

- **90% or higher favorable responses on Avatar Physician Satisfaction Survey** (a measurement tool administered by an independent third party) for 4 consecutive years, as well as a physician loyalty score in the national 99th percentile the year it received the Baldrige Award, as measured by Gallup (Poudre Valley Health System)

Reduction in Days in Accounts Receivable and Patient Length of Stay[a]

- **57% overall decline in net days in accounts receivable** over 3 years (Saint Luke's Hospital of Kansas City); **24% overall decline in net days in accounts receivable** over 5 years (Mercy Health System); **22% overall decline in net days in accounts receivable** over 4 years (North Mississippi Medical Center)

- **25% overall decline in gross days in accounts receivable** over 2 years (Bronson Methodist Hospital)

- **Nearly 28% overall improvement in length of stay** (Medicare) over 3 years (Poudre Valley Health System); **nearly 16% overall improvement** in length of stay (Medicare) over 4 years (AtlantiCare)

[a]Reducing length of stay, a common health-care sector quality measure, reduces hospital costs and also may reduce a patient's risk of hospital-acquired infections.

Increasing Training and Volunteer Hours

- **260% increase in training hours per full-time equivalent (FTE)** over 3 years (Bronson Methodist Hospital)

- **163% increase in training hours** over 6 years (Mercy Health System); **nearly 11% increase in training hours** over 2 years (SSM Health Care)

- **Nearly 44% increase in training hours per FTE** over 2 years (North Mississippi Medical Center)

- **225% increase in community-donated volunteer hours** over 4 years (Robert Wood Johnson University Hospital Hamilton)

- **86% increase in community-donated volunteer hours** over 2 years (Bronson Methodist Hospital)

Increasing Charity Care[a]

- **An increase of more than 50% in charity and uncompensated care** over 3 years (Heartland Health)

- **More than $181 million in community benefits**, including under- and uncompensated care, provided in the year before it received the Baldrige Award (Sharp HealthCare)

- **7% percent of total revenues donated to indigent care** in the year the organization received the Baldrige Award. The organization and its parent are the **leading providers of uncompensated care** in their market area. (Baptist Hospital, Inc.)

- **$62 million in unreimbursed care** for patients enrolled in government-assistance programs absorbed and **$1.9 million in charity care provided** in the 2 years before the organization received the Baldrige Award (Poudre Valley Health System)

- **56% of the previous year's operating margin allocated to the care of people who cannot pay,** in the year the organization received the Baldrige Award (SSM Health Care)

- **49% increase in uncompensated care costs as a percentage of total expenses** over 3 years; **more than $58 million in uncompensated care** provided in the year before the organization received the Baldrige Award (North Mississippi Medical Center)

- **88% increase in charity care** over 5 years; **1.8% of hospital and 2% of its clinic revenue allocated to charity care** in the year the organization received the Baldrige Award (Mercy Health System)

- **90% of the free care in its county** provided in the year before the organization received the Baldrige Award; **25% increase in free care** provided at cost over 4 years at AtlantiCare Regional Medical Center (AtlantiCare)

[a]Increasing charity care may be one way that hospitals demonstrate how they support their key communities.

The Case for Baldrige:
Role Models in Education

K-12

"Baldrige [offers] the only education Criteria that actually [enable a school system] to compare itself against other organizations . . . that show you what world-class looks like."

Dr. Terry Holliday, Superintendent (2002–2009)
Iredell-Statesville Schools
2008 Baldrige Award winner

Iredell-Statesville Schools (I-SS) is a kindergarten-through-12th-grade (K-12) public school system located in southwestern North Carolina. Although I-SS's budget and per-pupil expenditures ranked 107 of 115 districts in North Carolina, the district outperformed comparative districts in academics at the state and national levels.

I-SS supports its vision to "improve student learning" through its core values focusing on student learning, continuous improvement, management by fact, and results. Use of the Baldrige Criteria has promoted fact-based, data-driven decision making to support learning and continuous improvement throughout the school system.

Several years before receiving the Baldrige Award, I-SS began to use a Plan-Do-Study-Act (PDSA) process districtwide to raise students' SAT scores. When scores do not meet targets, the district uses the PDSA cycle to identify improvement opportunities and implement changes. Staff members review class and individual student data, assess progress toward goals, and modify improvement plans. As a result of the focus on continuous improvement, SAT scores in the district (shown in the figure below) steadily increased, outperforming average peer district, state, and national scores. The district's

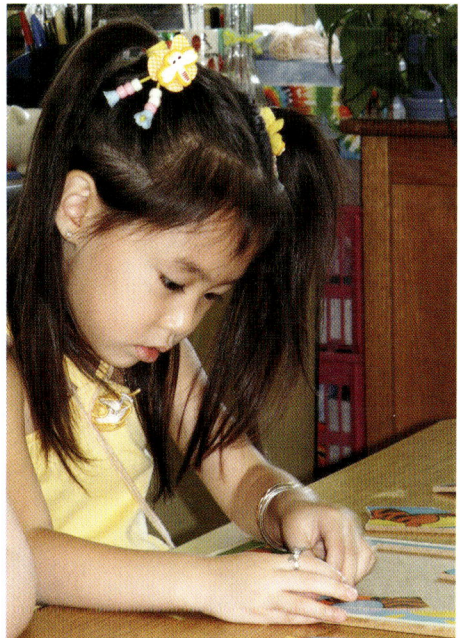

High School SAT Test Scores

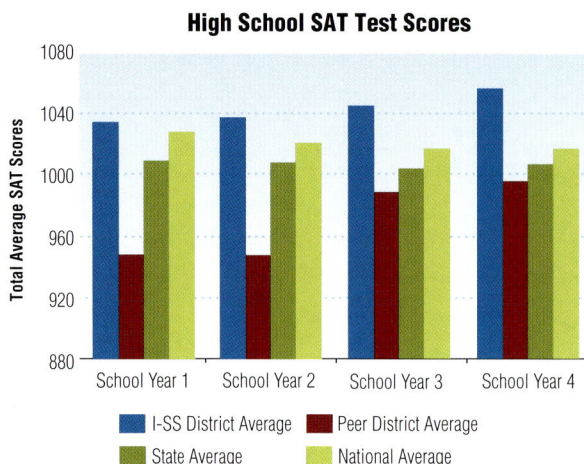

total average SAT score of 1056 in 2008 was better than that of the peer district (995), the state (1007), and the nation (1017). In addition, in the years preceding I-SS's receipt of the Baldrige Award, 29 percent of students scored 3 or higher on at least one Advanced Placement (AP) exam during high school, almost double the national rate.

I-SS also saw strong improvements in overall student achievement and reading. Over six years, I-SS rose from 55th to 9th place in student achievement among North Carolina's more than 100 school districts. The year before receiving the Baldrige Award, the district's students achieved 90.6 percent proficiency on the state reading assessment and narrowed the reading proficiency gap between African-American children and all students from 23 percent to 12.3 percent. The reading proficiency gap between exceptional children and all students decreased from 42 percent to 21 percent during the same period. In closing these gaps, I-SS outperformed other districts in the state.

Other results of I-SS's improvement journey include increases in the graduation rate from 61 percent to 81 percent (ranking I-SS 11th in North Carolina) and in the average SAT score from 991 to 1056 (ranking I-SS 7th in North Carolina), as well as a dropout rate that improved from one of the worst to one of the ten best in the state.

Higher Education

"This presidential recognition honors Richland College's serious commitment to and passion for student learning success and our vital mission of teaching, learning, and building a sustainable local and world community."

Dr. Stephen K. Mittelstet, President (1979–2009)
Richland College
2005 Baldrige Award winner

Richland College is a two-year community college in Dallas, Texas. Established in 1972, the college serves a culturally diverse student body that includes approximately 14,500 students pursuing college credits and nearly 6,000 continuing-education students. Richland College employs nearly 150 full-time faculty, more than 400 full-time support staff members and administrators, and 811 part-time faculty members. In 2005, it became the first community college to receive the Baldrige Award.

Richland College's mission—conveyed in the statement "Teaching, Learning, Community Building"—is to offer programs and services that enable its students to achieve their educational goals and become lifelong learners, community builders, and global citizens. Unlike peer community colleges, Richland College designs the bulk of its programs and services to meet the needs of students who intend to further their education at a four-year college or university. A measure of the college's success is thus the number of students who complete the core curriculum they need for transfer to four-year institutions. This number grew from 500 to 1,660 over three years, outperforming three of Richland's peer

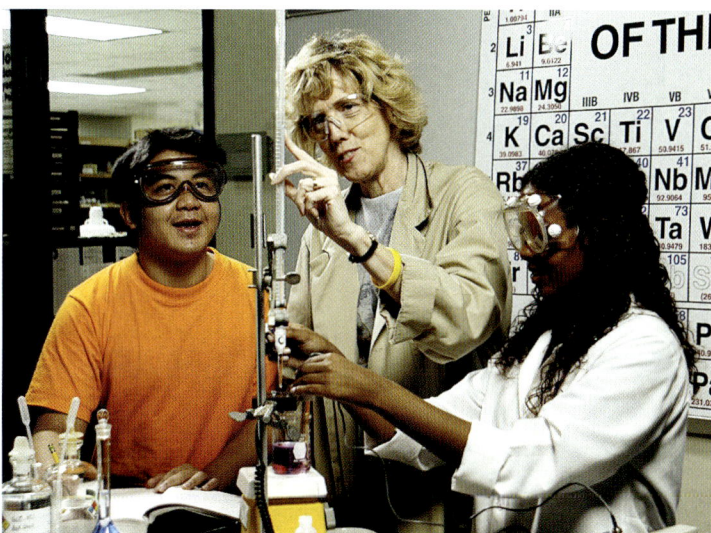

colleges. In addition, in the five years before Richland received the Baldrige Award, the number of credit students enrolled increased by approximately 16 percent, a growth rate that was higher than that for all local competitors in each of the five years. At the same time, on the four satisfaction measures that students rated as most important—related to class scheduling, class time convenience, variety of courses, and intellectual growth—Richland College surpassed the norm on the national Noel Levitz Student Satisfaction Survey over several consecutive years.

To make getting an education as convenient as possible for its students (with an average age of 28), Richland College offered alternatives to traditional classroom scheduling, including online, flex-term, and fast-track classes and evening and weekend courses. The college also maintains a close relationship with the local business community to ensure that its technical, occupational, and workforce job skills programs meet both students' needs and local employers' needs for a skilled workforce.

As another indicator of the success of the college and its students, the employment rate for students taking technical training or workforce development classes remained at or near 100 percent for the seven years before Richland College received the Baldrige Award. In an effort to improve its own and its peers' results, the college helped establish and participates in organizations such as the League for Innovation in the Community College and the Continuous Quality Improvement Network.

The Proof Is in the Data, Part 5:
The Baldrige Effect on Education

Since 2001, when the first organizations received the Baldrige Award in the education category, nine organizations have been so honored; six are public school districts:

- a K-12th-grade public school program located 20 miles north of New York City
- an Alaska standards-based program from preschool to beyond high school graduation that teaches students scattered throughout 22,000 square miles of isolated and remote areas
- a university in the University of Wisconsin System
- a K-8th-grade public school system in a northwestern Chicago suburb
- an undergraduate-only business school within the University of Northern Colorado
- a school district in Oklahoma that serves pre-K-12th-grade students
- a community college in the Dallas County Community College District
- a K-12th-grade public school system located in southwestern North Carolina
- a large, ethnically diverse K-12th-grade public school system in a Maryland suburb of Washington, D.C.

In the years leading up to role-model recognition as Baldrige Award winners, these districts and institutions achieved very favorable results that directly improved reading and mathematics proficiency, graduation rates, and turnover, as well as other measures. These achievements are highlighted below.

HIGH AND RISING
READING PROFICIENCY (K-12)

Reading Proficiency Rates[a]

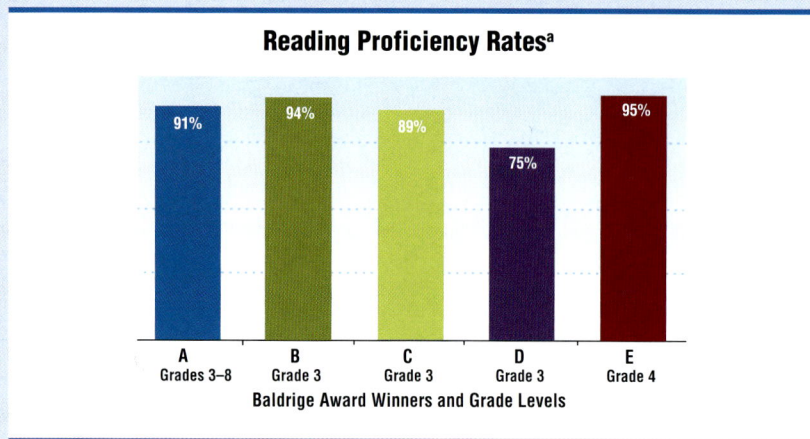

A	B	C	D	E
91%	94%	89%	75%	95%
Grades 3–8	Grade 3	Grade 3	Grade 3	Grade 4

Baldrige Award Winners and Grade Levels

[a] One district did not publicly report a comparable measure; see note 6 below. The levels shown above reflect the last year reported by each school district before it received the Baldrige Award.

1. School District A closed the reading proficiency gap between African-American students and all students from 23% to 12% over 6 years and closed the gap between students with special needs and all students from 42% to 21% during the same period.

2. For 5 years, School District B saw a 6% average annual improvement in grade 3 reading proficiency.

3. Grade 3 reading proficiency improved in each of the 4 years before School District C received the Baldrige Award. That year, the district's grade 2 reading proficiency reached 84% against the national average of 50% and gained 10 percentage points over the previous 2 years.

4. School District D's average student scores in reading on a national standardized achievement test rose from the 28th to the 71st percentile over 4 years. In addition, its average scores in language arts for the test rose from the 26th to the 72nd percentile over the same period.

5. School District E's grade 4 English/language arts proficiency rate averaged 96% for 6 consecutive years.

6. While the sixth district to win the Baldrige Award to date did not include a similar measure on reading proficiency in its award

application, it reported that it exceeded the required proficiency rate in reading for all school levels and doubled the percentage of grade 3 students scoring at the "advanced" level on state reading assessments from 14% to 28% over the 6 years leading up to its Baldrige Award.

High and Rising Mathematics Proficiency (K-12)

- **Average annual proficiency rate of 85%** on a composite grades 3–8 measure of reading and mathematics for 5 years (Iredell-Statesville Schools [I-SS])

- **Average annual proficiency rate of 98%** on a grade 4 mathematics measure for 5 years (Pearl River School District)

- **92% of grade 3 students meeting or exceeding Illinois Standards Achievement Test standards** in mathematics (Community Consolidated School District 15)

- **11% average annual improvement** for 5 years on a composite K-12 mathematics proficiency measure (Chugach School District)

- **94% proficiency rate** on a grade 8 mathematics measure, with a **2% average annual improvement** for 5 years (Jenks Public Schools)

High and Rising AP Enrollment and Exam Scores (K-12)

- **More than 66% of high school graduates (Class of 2010) took at least one AP course and exam**, compared with 28.3% nationally and 43.4% in other districts in the state of Maryland; **scores of "3" or higher were earned by 50%** of these students, compared to 16.9% nationally and 26.4% statewide. Plus, over the decade preceding this district's Baldrige Award, **the number of AP exams taken by its high school students more than tripled and the number of AP exams they took that earned scores of "3" or higher more than doubled.** (Montgomery County Public Schools)

- **Nearly 60% of grade 12 students took at least one AP course; scores of "3" or better were earned by 76%** of those taking AP tests the year the district won the Baldrige Award. (Pearl River School District)

- Increase from **12.5% to 43.8% in student enrollment in AP courses** (% of student body enrolled in at least one AP course), compared to 31% nationally; **scores of "3" or higher were earned on 62% to 67% of AP tests taken,** and **37% of all grade 12 students had earned an AP test score of "3" or better**, compared to 13% nationally, in the year leading up to the district's Baldrige Award (Jenks Public Schools)

High and Rising Graduation Rates and College Attendance (K-12)

- **More than 60% of graduates earned a four-year college degree** within 6 years (Classes of 2001 and 2003). Plus, in the year this district won the Baldrige Award, it boasted the **highest graduation rate of any large school district in the nation**, according to an *Education Week* study. (Montgomery County Public Schools)

- **7% average annual improvement in cohort graduation rate** (% of students entering grade 9 who graduate 4 years later) for 4 years, from nearly 64% to 81% (I-SS)

- **93% to 95% graduation rate** (% of students entering grade 12 who graduate that year) sustained over 3 years (Jenks Public Schools)

- **100% graduation rate** (% of students entering grade 12 who graduate that year) for 5 years, **a 7% average annual increase** in students graduating with a Regents diploma (Pearl River School District)

- **A 6-year improvement in the dropout rate from among the worst in the state to among the best** (3.5%) for students in grades 9–12 (I-SS)

- **Results higher than the state average in 4 subject areas** on Alaska's High School Graduation Qualifying Exam (Chugach School District)

- **9% average annual growth in the number of graduates attending college after graduation** over 6 years; **96% of graduates attending college immediately after matriculation,** and **100% doing so within 5 years** of graduating from high school (Pearl River School District)

SUCCESS AFTER GRADUATION (COLLEGIATE)

Graduate Employment Rates after College[a]

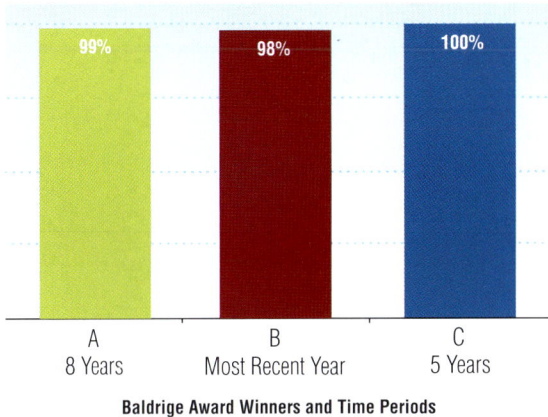

Bar chart showing:
- A / 8 Years: 99%
- B / Most Recent Year: 98%
- C / 5 Years: 100%

Baldrige Award Winners and Time Periods

[a]The levels shown above reflect the most recent time periods reported by each institution before it received the Baldrige Award.

1. Institution A, a community college, achieved a 100% employment rate for technical training/workforce development students and sustained this rate for 8 years.

2. Institution B, an undergraduate college of business, achieved a 98% employment or graduate school attendance rate by recent graduates, and more than 90% of organizations employing graduates rated the program as good or excellent.

3. Institution C, a four-year public university, achieved a 98% job-placement rate for recent graduates and sustained this average rate for 5 years.

High and Rising Student Satisfaction (Collegiate)

- **Top 10% ranking nationally on 10 of 16 student satisfaction measures** on student surveys by Educational Benchmarking, Inc. (EBI); for 2 years, **scores in the top 1% for overall student satisfaction** (Kenneth W. Monfort College of Business)

- **For 5 years, ranked in the top 10% of 171 schools** included in the EBI survey for students' rating of the value of their investment in their degree; **tuition and fees 39% lower** than the national average (Kenneth W. Monfort College of Business)

- Survey **results above the national norm on 4 of its 5 most important measures of student satisfaction** and on **42 of 79 survey items** (Richland College)

LOW AND DECREASING TEACHER TURNOVER

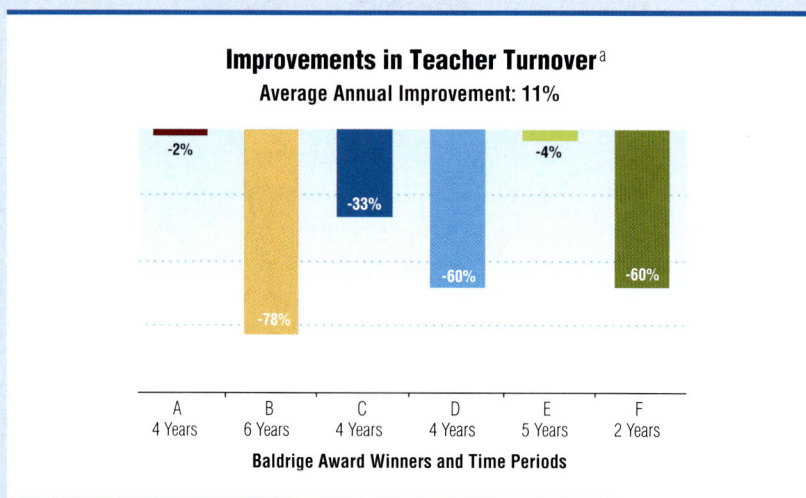

Improvements in Teacher Turnover[a]

Average Annual Improvement: 11%

-2%		-33%		-4%	
	-78%		-60%		-60%

A	B	C	D	E	F
4 Years	6 Years	4 Years	4 Years	5 Years	2 Years

Baldrige Award Winners and Time Periods

[a]The improvements shown above reflect the most recent time periods reported by each school district before it received the Baldrige Award.

1. School District A's turnover rate for the last year reported in its Baldrige Award application was 12% compared with a national average of 20%.

2. School District D's certified staff turnover rate for the last year reported was 6%, compared to a national rate of 20% that year.

3. School District E decreased its turnover rate to below the state average. The district started the last school year reported with 100% of staff positions filled and waiting lists for most job openings.

4. School District F's teacher turnover rate for the last year reported was 4.6%, compared to a national average of 16.8% that year.

- **Voluntary faculty turnover rate of about 3% or less** for 6 years (University of Wisconsin–Stout)

- **Overall turnover rate of 8%** over 5 years (Richland College)

High and Rising Faculty and Staff Satisfaction

- **4% average annual improvement rate** for the 3 2000–2009 Baldrige Award-winning school districts and 3 collegiate institutions reporting such data.

- **Over 90% teacher satisfaction rate** reported across elementary, middle, and high school levels for 3 years leading up to this district's Baldrige Award; for employees at all school levels, favorable responses to survey questions regarding **work satisfaction ranged from 91.3% to 95.5%**, and favorable responses from non-school-based employees increased from 78.9% to 84.8% over the same time period. (Montgomery County Public Schools)

- Over 3 years, improvement **from an average satisfaction rating of 3.67 on a 5-point scale to 4.00** for all employees, based on exit interviews (University of Wisconsin–Stout)

- Improvement in the levels of employee enthusiasm for work from **an average rating of 3.64 on a 5-point scale to an average rating of 4.62, a 27% improvement** in 3 surveys over a 7-year period (Jenks Public Schools)

- **97% satisfaction rate** among faculty and staff, up from 88% for the combined group of faculty and staff segments 3 years earlier; this score **served as the benchmark** for schools using the same survey. (Pearl River School District)

The Case for Baldrige:
Successes in the Nonprofit Sector

Municipal Government

"The real value in applying for this Award is in the rigorous evaluation process. The constructive feedback from Baldrige helps us improve the way we do business."

Mike Levinson, City Manager (1993–2010)
City of Coral Springs
2007 Baldrige Award winner

Chartered in 1963 and once known as the "City in the Country," the city of **Coral Springs** is located in Broward County, southern Florida. During the 1980s, Coral Springs was one of the fastest-growing cities in the nation and was home to about 132,000 people in 2006, making it the 13th-largest city in the state. With an annual budget of $135 million as of 2007, the city of Coral Springs has a council-manager form of government: the City Commission serves as the board of directors, and the city manager as chief executive officer, with input from citizens and businesses.

Coral Springs is a role model in its focus on customers and boasts high satisfaction rates as a result. For the seven years before it received the Baldrige Award, the city's overall quality ratings were higher than 90 percent, which surpassed International City/County Management Association (ICMA) comparison cities. The percentage of residents who were satisfied with city services was in the mid- to upper 90s. Business owners in Coral Springs who were satisfied with the city increased

from 76 percent to 97 percent over three years, and 90 percent of business owners said they would recommend the city to others—compared with the American Customer Satisfaction Index national average of about 75 percent. In addition, the year before it received the Baldrige Award, the city's millage rate—the amount per $1,000 that is used to calculate property taxes—was the lowest of all cities in Broward County. In 2006, *Money* magazine named Coral Springs among the "Best Places to Live," and in 2005, 2006, and 2007, the city was named one of the 100 best communities for young people by America's Promise Alliance.

Coral Springs managed to satisfy residents and businesses while maintaining a strong balance sheet and cash position. For seven straight years, the city attained a "AAA" rating from the nation's three largest bond-rating agencies—Moody's Investor Services, Standard and Poor's, and Fitch.

Coral Springs Quality Ratings

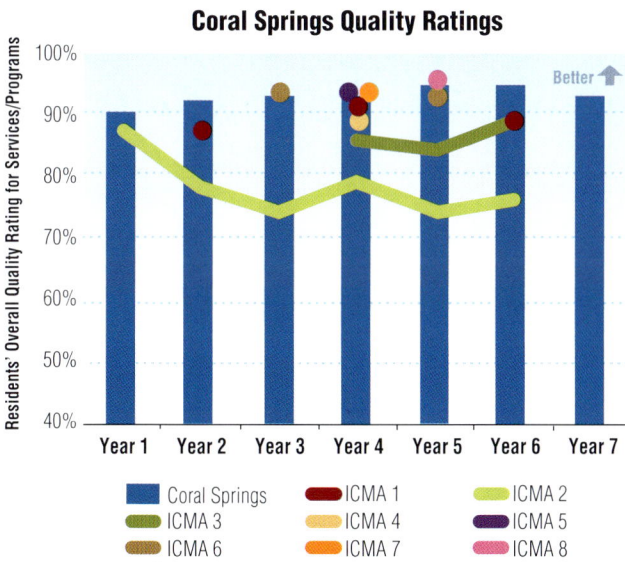

U.S. Military

"[The men and women of ARDEC] have earned distinction for our organization, the new high-technology Army, and the Department of Defense by embracing the Baldrige Criteria. . . . We [adopted the Baldrige Criteria] in order to become the best organization we can possibly be and provide the best products and support we can to the U.S. Warfighter."

Dr. Joseph A. Lannon, Director
U.S. Army Armament Research, Development and Engineering Center (ARDEC)
2007 Baldrige Award winner

The **U.S. Army Armament Research, Development and Engineering Center (ARDEC)** is a specialized center within the U.S. Army Materiel Command. ARDEC develops 90 percent of the Army's armaments and ammunition, including warheads, explosives, all sizes of firearms, battlefield sensors, and advanced weaponry based on high-power microwaves, high-energy lasers, and nanotechnology.

A 2007 Baldrige Award winner, ARDEC has demonstrated strong financial results. Its overall revenue increased from $640 million to over $1 billion in six years. In the same period, revenue from non-Army customers (from other government agencies [OGAs], the Defense Advanced Research Projects Agency [DARPA], and Cooperative Research and Development Agreements [CRADAs]) grew from $60 million to $140 million. ARDEC's revenues continued to increase as a direct result of its Enterprise Excellence initiative, including its Strategic Management System. The continuous upward trend in non-Army funding shown in the figure on the next page demonstrates how ARDEC has diversified its customers in light of the potential for constrained Army budgets in the future.

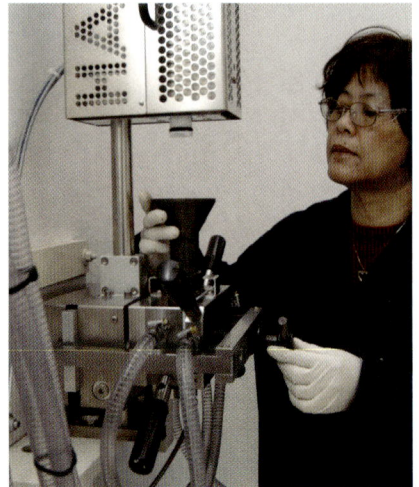

Non-Army Revenue & Percentage of Total ARDEC Revenue

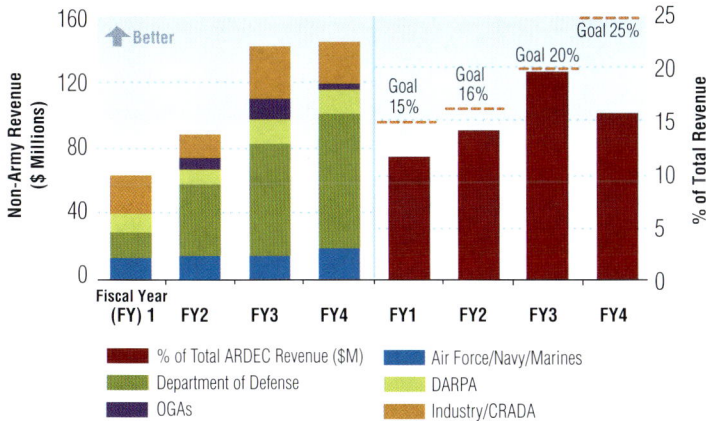

Legend:
- % of Total ARDEC Revenue ($M)
- Department of Defense
- OGAs
- Air Force/Navy/Marines
- DARPA
- Industry/CRADA

ARDEC's overall customer satisfaction rating increased from 3.48 (on a 4-point scale) to 3.75 over six years, exceeding both government and industry benchmarks. For a three-year period, satisfaction among Army customers remained fairly consistent at 3.62, while satisfaction among non-Army customers increased from 3.82 to 3.92. This success grew largely out of ARDEC's method of gathering and using information from its customers. Web-based customer satisfaction surveys provide 1,500 data points and over 60 pages of comments each quarter, with the results available to everyone in the workforce.

ARDEC also has developed a number of tools to help it react quickly and effectively to customers' needs. For example, the center formalized a Web-based tool for collecting and tracking customer requests with the objective to close all requests within 72 hours. ARDEC met that goal in five of six quarters starting the year after the tool was introduced.

The Proof Is in the Data, Part 6:
The Baldrige Effect on Nonprofits

Since 2007, when the first organization received the Baldrige Award in the nonprofit category, three organizations have been so honored:

- the 13th-largest city in the state of Florida
- a center within the U.S. Army Materiel Command that develops 90% of the Army's armaments and ammunition
- a federal government organization that supports multicenter clinical trials targeting current health issues for America's veterans

In the years leading up to recognition as Baldrige Award winners, these organizations achieved very favorable results that directly improved customer satisfaction, financial results, and employee turnover, as well as other measures. These achievements are highlighted below.

SATISFIED CUSTOMERS

Customer Satisfaction Levels[a]

A	B Customer Group 1	B Customer Group 2	C
94%	97%	93%	100%

Baldrige Award Winners

[a]The levels shown above reflect the last year reported by each organization before it received the Baldrige Award.

1. For Nonprofit Organization A, customer satisfaction increased 8% over 7 years.

2. For its customer group 1, Nonprofit Organization B reported a 28% gain in customer satisfaction over 3 years.

Baldrige 20/20: An Executive's Guide to the Criteria for Performance Excellence

3. For its customer group 2, Nonprofit Organization B reported customer satisfaction of 92% or higher for 9 consecutive years.

4. For Nonprofit Organization C, customer satisfaction increased 20% over 6 years.

- **90% of businesses would recommend** the city as a place to do business, a **13% gain** over 3 years. (City of Coral Springs)

- **75% of customer relationships were longer than 10 years.** (Veterans Affairs Cooperative Studies Program Clinical Research Pharmacy Coordinating Center [the Center])

- **For 6 years, fewer than 1% of customers reported dissatisfaction.** (U.S. Army Armament Research, Development and Engineering Center [ARDEC])

Improved Financial Results

- **56% increase in revenue** over 6 years (ARDEC)

- **Cost avoidance of $3.22 billion** over 5 years (ARDEC)

- **Budget growth of 143%** over 6 years (the Center)

- **99% or greater performance to budget** over 6 years (the Center)

A SATISFIED, STABLE WORKFORCE

Workforce Satisfaction Increases[a]
Average Annual Improvement: 3%

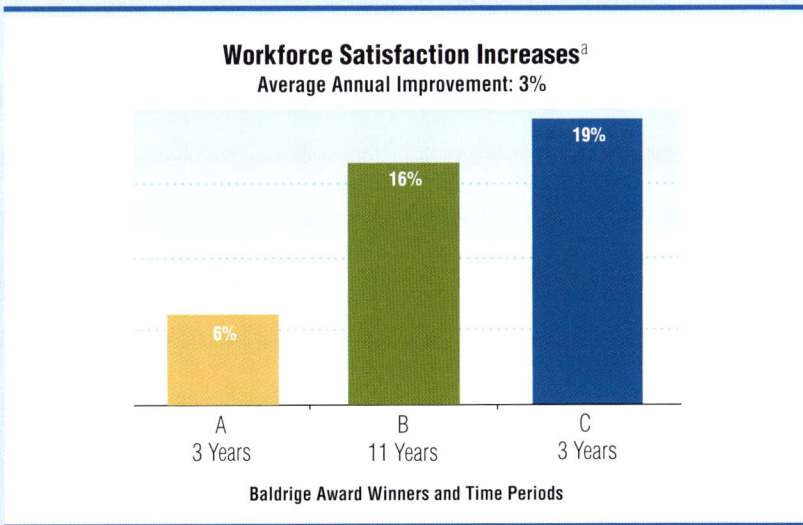

A 3 Years	B 11 Years	C 3 Years
6%	16%	19%

Baldrige Award Winners and Time Periods

[a]The improvements shown above reflect the most recent time periods reported by each organization before it received the Baldrige Award.

- **53% decrease in employee turnover** over 9 years (City of Coral Springs)

- **29% decrease in employee turnover** over 7 years (the Center)

- **95% employee satisfaction** against an average of 60% to 65% on the Federal Human Capital Survey in the year the Baldrige Award was received (City of Coral Springs)

Excellent Service

- **50% decrease in crime rate** over 10 years (City of Coral Springs)

- **100% of complaints closed** within 7 business days (City of Coral Springs)

- **50% increase in product releases** over 5 years (ARDEC)

- **Less than 1 complaint per million units delivered** in 8 of 9 years (the Center)

What NOT to do in preparing a Baldrige Award application!

The Dilbert comic strip spoofed the Baldrige Program in the mid-1990s.

DILBERT: © Scott Adams/Dist. by United Feature Syndicate, Inc.

Award Winners' Journeys: How Baldrige Led Them to Excellence

The journeys that Malcolm Baldrige National Quality Award winners take to attain performance excellence may vary, but the results are the same: recognition as best-in-class, world-class, and national role models. The stories in this section recount Baldrige Award winners' strategies for continuous improvement and the determination that led to excellence. In each case, an executive determined that the Baldrige framework—the Criteria for Performance Excellence—was not just a way to foster innovation and run the business, but *the* way to achieve success and sustainability.

Each story is followed by the lessons these executives learned as they negotiated the turning points on their journeys to excellence. Here are some common themes:

- Be willing to accept feedback and strive for incremental improvement while also addressing opportunities for breakthrough innovation.

- Engage your organization's senior leaders in the journey.

- Listen to and integrate the voice of the customer into your products and processes.

- Focus on beneficial results rather than on winning the Baldrige Award.

- Never lose sight that your organization is improving even if you haven't achieved your ultimate goals.

- Focus on relationships and building trust.

- Determine what level of performance your organization wishes to achieve and what type of evidence you need to collect to prove that you have achieved it.

From Kernel to Crystal

Cargill Corn Milling (CCM) could not have reached its level of performance excellence without the Baldrige Criteria, says Ron Fiala, process improvement manager of the 2008 Baldrige Award winner. The Criteria helped CCM see that the elements critical to its success are (1) leadership involvement and support, (2) relentless determination, (3) internal and external intellectual and cultural resources (such as state and local Baldrige-based award programs and the national Baldrige Program), and (4) the wherewithal to accept feedback. These are all elements of the Baldrige Criteria for Performance Excellence.

CCM was established over 40 years ago, when its parent company, Cargill, Inc., acquired a small plant in Cedar Rapids, Iowa, that processed about 10,000 bushels of corn a day, or approximately 12 truckloads. Today, CCM operates nine plants and processes over 1 million bushels of corn each day. That's equivalent to the yield of a cornfield the size of the state of Connecticut every year.

To accommodate rapid increases in customers and product offerings, CCM had to grow. But this growth could not be just about continuous expansion, says Fiala. It was critical to focus on continuous improvement. CCM needed to improve its process control and ability to make high-quality products. CCM's early business model was to run each plant as a separate company, with its own profit-and-loss statement. The plants competed not only with outside companies but also with other CCM plants.

According to Fiala, CCM, like many manufacturing companies, started its total quality efforts in the mid-1980s because of customer requirements for product quality. In 1991, Cargill's Corporate Quality Department created the internal Chairman's Quality Award, which singled out the best-run plants in the company; the award criteria were based on the Baldrige Criteria. Applying to and receiving feedback from this internal award program helped CCM embed its process orientation into its culture. During this period, CCM was one of the most successful Cargill businesses; however, nothing lasts forever, especially in business.

A Group of Plants or an Enterprise?

After years of scrambling to keep up with growing demand, CCM faced overcapacity, says Fiala. This flip-flop in supply and demand caused syrup prices to plummet to record low levels. Everyone in the corn milling industry suffered, which led to several consolidations among competitors. This led to overcapacity in the marketplace, and CCM needed to reevaluate how it operated.

The biggest difference between CCM and its competitors, Fiala says, was that it operated more plants in more locations. This difference could be a huge benefit if CCM could tap into the skills, knowledge, and ideas of all of its employees at every location and effectively share across plants. To accomplish this, CCM had to shift from being plant-centric to operating all plants as a single enterprise. From then on, only one bottom line would matter—that of the business as a whole, Fiala says. Adopting the Baldrige Criteria, with its holistic, systems framework, became the logical next step, and CCM began actively incorporating more Criteria concepts into its own practices, including the formation of best-practice teams and the sharing of learning across all plants.

The Defining Moment

At about the same time, Cargill's internal award was renamed the Business Excellence Award, with the Baldrige Criteria remaining its foundation. The biggest change to the internal award, according to Fiala, was that CCM could only apply as an enterprise; individual plants within CCM could not apply. CCM submitted an application, and Fiala and his colleagues were shocked when it scored poorly. CCM protested that the process must have been flawed, and its objections went all the way to the president of Cargill, Greg Page, who agreed to spend one entire day reviewing CCM's award application. Apparently, Page did not believe CCM's protest was legitimate. He simply said, "If you truly think you are better than this score indicates, then get to work and prove it!"

This was the defining moment in CCM's journey, Fiala says. "It took us a while, but we finally did accept the feedback to more systematically deploy processes across our plants." From that point on, CCM wholeheartedly adopted the Baldrige Criteria: The company refined its strategy review process to make it more systematic and involve additional employees, and it created expert panels to integrate the voice of the customer into operations. That all CCM employees understand "how they fit and why they matter" became a goal, says Fiala. The best-practice model was improved to systematically identify, measure, document, and implement best practices, and the company put an innovation process in place to collect, track, and implement great ideas from all employees. Thus, CCM moved from merely focusing on continuous improvement to fostering innovation at the same time.

In the fall of 2005, CCM's leaders, desiring additional feedback about its processes from outside Cargill, decided to apply for the national Baldrige Award. Fiala says the feedback contained some excellent recommendations, and executives used the feedback to create the Corn Milling Leadership System, which incorporates all aspects of the Baldrige Criteria. In 2008, CCM received the Malcolm Baldrige National Quality Award.

CCM's ability to execute its strategy enabled it to increase its profitability in the ten years before it received the Baldrige Award. "We believe even in today's tough economic environment, that our people and our systematic processes will help us weather the storm," Fiala says.

DOs AND DON'Ts

Don't expect only highs along the journey. Executives must be willing to make incremental improvements every day.

Don't reject external feedback without giving it due consideration. The hardest part about feedback is having the courage to accept it.

Do make the decision to truly become a process-honoring culture. In 2002, CCM made this decision, which became a defining moment.

Do accept that an outside set of eyes can point out your blind spots.

Do recognize the elements critical to success: leadership involvement and support, determination, resources (both internal and external), and willingness to accept feedback.

A Return from the Brink

According to CEO Rulon Stacey, **Poudre Valley Health System (PVHS)** began its Baldrige journey in the mid-1990s, when it was a community hospital serving only Fort Collins, Colorado. The hospital faced an employee turnover rate of 25 percent each year and had been led by a succession of five CEOs in four years. PVHS's annual revenues were a quarter of what they had been in recent years, and the local health care market was demanding more integration with physicians. It was a critical time for the organization, says Stacey, as it needed a process that would allow it to set its sights high and continually improve.

In 1997, with the support of the Board of Directors, executives began a review of different tools that supported continuous improvement in patient care; PVHS chose the Baldrige Criteria for Performance Excellence.

PVHS first submitted a Baldrige application in 2000, after convening teams focused on each of the seven Criteria categories. Each team wrote its own section of the application, and "we stuck these sections together," Stacey says. Initially, he added, the Baldrige effort

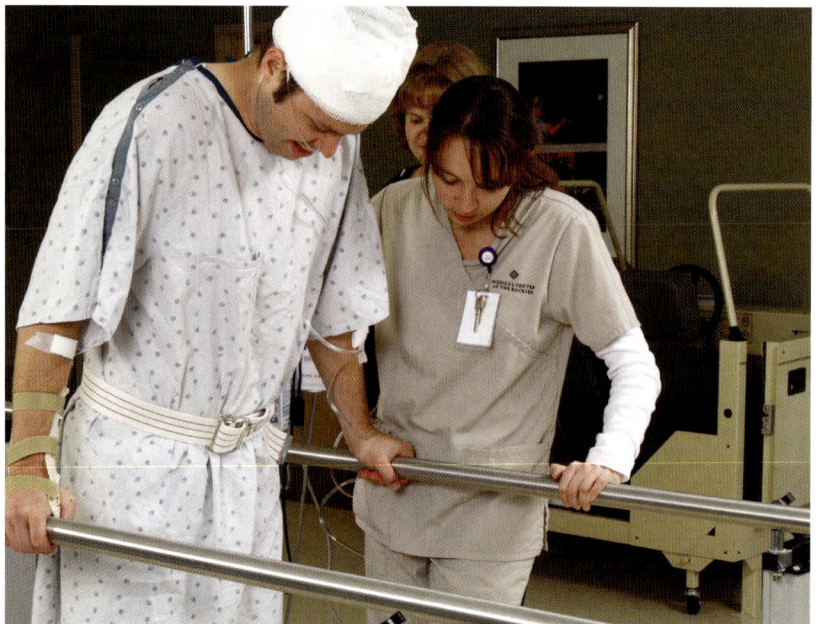

was something employees worked on once a year, outside their "real jobs," and they looked only at their assigned categories.

Still, Stacey says, PVHS really expected to "win" the Baldrige Award early on. "We were used to winning awards, and certainly, we thought, Baldrige was no different. . . . We were quite shocked to get our first feedback report and find we were only in Scoring Band 2 [out of 8]."

A New Approach: Systematic Improvement

The year 2004 was a turning point. As Stacey explains, PVHS realized that for Baldrige to work for the organization, it needed to make Baldrige "how it does business." First, PVHS created a Quality Improvement Department to establish a systematic and integrated approach to performance excellence that crossed calendars and Criteria categories. Then seven performance excellence teams were trained on the Baldrige Criteria categories and worked to identify gaps in the organization. Senior leaders served either as team leaders or as team members. Teams also included people from across facilities, disciplines, and customer groups.

Stacey says that, each year, PVHS rigorously assessed its progress through the Baldrige application process and the feedback report it received. Senior leaders reviewed the reports and set the direction for the seven performance excellence teams. The teams each developed an annual action plan detailing improvements to work on during the year ahead. The Quality Improvement Department then worked with each of the performance excellence teams to develop an action plan aligned with the organization's strategic plan.

According to Stacey, in response to Baldrige feedback, the Leadership Team has been instrumental in deploying PVHS's vision, mission, and values across the organization through its Global Path to Success system. In addition, the team set up a process for taking corrective action when systemwide balanced scorecard measures are not performing to goal. Thanks to the Strategy Team's numerous cycles of improvement, the strategic planning timeline was aligned with leadership retreats and the capital and operational budget

> "A common question we get is, how much productive time do you lose to Baldrige? If you're asking that question, you don't get it yet. Baldrige has to be how you run your business. . . . People want to know how we can afford to do Baldrige. We tell them, 'You can't afford not to.'"
>
> —Poudre Valley Health System CEO Rulon Stacey

cycles. This team also rolled out personal goal cards as a way of linking individual employees' actions to the organization's strategic objectives. And the team continues to work on new ways to involve physicians in strategic planning.

Based on Baldrige feedback, PVHS now has a systematic approach to tracking, trending, and sharing the voice of the customer to determine how the organization is doing in customer service and where it can improve. PVHS also changed the way it looks at patient satisfaction data. The Knowledge Management Team continues to refine the balanced scorecard process, adding definition sheets that standardize what PVHS is measuring and how it is measured. This team also led the transition to an electronic balanced scorecard and to the use of a national database for risk- and severity-adjusted clinical outcomes. The Workforce Team established and deployed behavior standards, launched "stay" interviews with current employees (moving away from "exit" interviews with departing employees), instituted performance reviews for volunteers, and expanded a peer-to-peer coupon program ($3 coupons for the gift shop, local businesses, and cafeteria that peers award each other for actions supporting standards and values) to include volunteers and physicians. The Process Improvement Team established the Business Decision Support Process to analyze and prioritize proposals for new service offerings as well as major capital projects. Stacey says the overall result has been continuous, systematic improvement driven by the Baldrige Criteria.

In 2008, PVHS received the Baldrige Award. "Baldrige has paid off for us," says Stacey. But PVHS certainly does not consider its Baldrige journey over. Even as a Baldrige Award winner, PVHS found that its 2008 Baldrige feedback report included 32 opportunities for improvement, and the organization was already working on those it had identified even before the report arrived, he adds.

DOs AND DON'Ts

Don't let Baldrige become an activity your organization does on the side. As Stacey remembers it, "Initially, Baldrige was something people did once a year, looking at each category in a silo, separate from their 'real jobs.'" This approach did not work.

Don't overemphasize the award. At one point in PVHS's journey, says Stacey, "There was a perception among employees and physicians that this was just one more award we wanted to add to our résumé . . . [so] motivation dropped when we found out that we were not a winner." However, Stacey adds, "It was so much more motivational to engage our workforce in providing world-class care instead of asking for their help to win another award."

Don't give up. "There were lots of times in our journey when we questioned whether it was worth it," says Stacey. "We got disappointed, even angry, and staff seemed to lose motivation. But we persisted and focused on improvements we had already made and improvements we wanted to make."

Don't "cram for the test." Don't do Baldrige by simply memorizing the "right" answers before the Baldrige examiners visit your site as part of their evaluation, advises Stacey, "Live it!"

Do get buy-in from the top. As PVHS found, direction and empowerment from leadership is essential.

Do consider Baldrige-related activities productive time. "A common question we get is, how much productive time do you lose to Baldrige?" says Stacey. "If you're asking that question, you don't get it yet. Baldrige has to be how you run your business."

Do make improvement your main focus. Says Stacey, "We realized that a lot of our focus had shifted to 'winning the award.'" When the main focus shifted back to improving, PVHS began seeing the beneficial results that led it to the Baldrige Award.

A Baldrige Cinderella Story

Terry May, CEO, president, and founder of **MESA Products, Inc.,** characterizes his small company's journey to performance excellence as a Cinderella story. Founded in 1979 with just a single client, MESA today is headquartered in Tulsa, Oklahoma, with five branch offices in Tallahassee, Florida; Houston, Texas; Huntington Beach, California; Fort Worth, Texas; and Wapakoneta, Ohio. The company provides engineering, installation, and materials for cathodic protection systems (a process that prevents metal structures, particularly underground hydrocarbon pipelines and tanks, from corroding).

> "One of the most interesting things we've learned from the whole Malcolm Baldrige experience is that when a company has a vision, a mission, and well-defined values, it has the foundation necessary to operate in any environment."
>
> —MESA CEO Terry May

Growth, Quality, and Difficulties

In MESA's early days, it focused on engineering and technical services. As the organization grew, May added installation services and materials. These expansions during a time when the industry was depressed allowed MESA to maintain steady, profitable growth. But May also wanted his company to deliver a "quality product at a fair price," so he focused on that concept throughout the company's first decade, despite the difficulties he faced in securing bank loans to keep the company operating.

"In the early eighties, we were always concerned about how we'd survive, but there was always some level of optimism," says May. "The turning point for us was one job that threw off a lot of cash. Once it looked to the banks that we didn't need the money, they were eager to loan it to us. That was the first time we could comfortably think we were going to make it." Then, in 1989, *Inc.* magazine recognized MESA in its "Top 500" list of the fastest-growing private companies in the United States.

As the company continued growing and taking on larger projects, May's frustration kept pace. "With all that going on, we started screwing up more. No big blunders, but by now, the cost of those mistakes was becoming greater and had more impact. That's when I first became interested in the formal concepts of quality," says May. He started reading books on quality and subsequently led

MESA through two unsuccessful attempts at Total Quality Management. Following successful implementation of ISO 9002 certification, May became aware of the Baldrige Award. In 2002, while on jury duty (during breaks) and equipped with a laptop and a Criteria booklet, May started typing responses to the Criteria questions. "By the time jury duty ended, I had 15 typewritten pages and figured, how much harder could it be to finish?" Working alone on nights and weekends, his subsequent quest to finish answering all the Criteria questions took him another 250 hours: "What was so appealing is that, from the Criteria, I saw many things that MESA was already doing or discussing—strategy, customer satisfaction, employee satisfaction, vision, values. Baldrige just seemed to wrap all that into one neat little package."

Getting Better with Each Feedback Report

A month after he submitted the application, May told his leadership team what he'd done. The response was, "What's Baldrige?" While MESA's leadership team didn't see the value yet, May says he saw it as an accomplishment that he'd told the entire MESA story in 35 pages. But he was not pleased when he received the feedback report written by a team of Baldrige examiners. May admits he was initially angered by the opportunities for improvement (known as OFIs) in the report, but after he reread them, he started to think the feedback could help his company. "After tossing out 30 percent of the OFIs because they had no immediate value to MESA," he recalls, he realized "there was value in what the report said."

In 2003, May got the rest of the MESA management involved in the Baldrige process, wrote another Baldrige Award application, and earned a site visit. But he says that his company was not prepared for that visit by Baldrige examiners. "We had a false sense of where we were," he says.

By 2004, MESA had addressed the OFIs from its previous feedback report, written another application, and earned another site visit. This time May involved almost everyone in the company in the process. "I was putting pressure on people, sending them to Baldrige training, and simultaneously applying for the Oklahoma Quality Award. But our Baldrige experience was a disaster."

In 2005, after addressing the new OFIs and writing another application, May and his company received another site visit, but it did not receive the Baldrige Award. "The feedback was that we'd improved, but we just weren't there yet," says May. On the positive side, he adds, everyone recognized the value of the process, as improvements were evident and producing results.

In 2006, after deepening the commitment of the senior management team to the Baldrige process and addressing the OFIs, MESA again submitted a Baldrige application and received a site visit. This time, the company finally received the Baldrige Award. In the same year, MESA also received the Oklahoma Quality Award.

May learned that being a Baldrige Award winner did not mean his company had reached the end of its improvement journey: "Along with the announcement that we'd won the Baldrige Award came another 50 OFIs," he says. "So we're addressing those and will continue to improve."

DOs and DON'Ts

Don't set expectations for a quick journey to performance excellence. MESA's early expectations were unrealistic, says May—a certain recipe for frustration, discouragement, and failure.

Don't focus just on winning an award. "Every year we didn't win, we'd still gotten better as a company," says May. He recommends focusing on the positives, addressing the OFIs in feedback reports, and never losing sight that the organization is improving throughout the journey.

Do things your way; there is no magic formula. "Our method was trial and error—and it took us five years," says May. "As a small company, our resources are limited. But although we may not do things the way others do, we find ways to get things done."

Do be patient, and do your best. One trick is not to call this process "Baldrige," says May. "We needed this to become part of our daily job, so we called what we were doing 'The MESA Way.'"

A Baldrige Transformation

Iredell-Statesville Schools (I-SS) was formed in 1992 from the merger of a county school system and a city school system. By the 2000-2001 school year, the school board had initiated an investigation of the low-performing school system based on reports of financial mismanagement. A posting on the school system's Web page subsequently made over 70 negative findings public. The Board of Education eventually fired the superintendent and conducted a search for a new one.

Terry Holliday was selected for the position in the fall of 2002. According to Holliday, the Board of Education offered him the job because of his Baldrige-based plan for turning around the system: "They said I was the only one who had 'a plan.' The plan I had presented to them was based on the Baldrige Criteria. The plan I presented was about changing the *system* from a teaching- and adult-centered system to a *learning*-based *system*."

At the start of Holliday's tenure, he says, "We had a school system that was broke, a budget that was about $2.5 million over revenue, below-state-average student achievement, low community expectations, a community that did not trust the school board or the superintendent, deteriorating school facilities, and a fast-growing population due to suburban sprawl."

However, Holliday embarked on the journey toward success for I-SS confident that he had the

resources he needed to address the challenges: "We did have one thing—great staff and a school board that wanted change!" He adds that the system's new vision was a key driver of the improvement journey. "Our vision that we adopted by the end of the first year was very simple and one that everyone could understand," says Holliday. "We wanted to become a 'top-ten' school system in North Carolina as measured by student learning outcomes."

From Blame to a Focus on Learning

At first, Holliday faced a clash of cultures: "Very quickly it became evident that there was an impending conflict between the leadership beliefs/values as espoused by the Baldrige Criteria and the existing culture in our community." The community of parents and teachers tended to blame others (especially the superintendent and school leaders) for failures, he says. In addition, the organizational culture focused on what was best for adults, not what was best for learning. "Decisions were often made according to 'that's the way we have always done it around here' rather than based on data," Holliday says. He also faced mistrust of new programs or innovations, such as the plan, do, study, act (PDSA) continuous improvement methodology, Holliday added.

Beginning the Baldrige journey "with a few strikes against us," Holliday knew it was extremely important that he, along with the Board of Education and other senior leaders, focus on a passion for learning, including the need to reignite this passion in adults. "I truly believe parents and teachers want all children to be successful. They just do not know how to help the children reach success. . . . We have to believe that we can ignite a passion for learning in everyone." He added, "Actions must reveal a focus on learning rather than a focus on adults by always looking at how we can help each other become more effective in helping more children learn."

As I-SS started its Baldrige journey, Holliday also knew that having everyone read the Criteria would not mean "they would instantly become systems thinkers and agents of change." Instead, he understood that he had to start with small changes and produce early successes to bring people along on the journey.

During the system's first six months of using the Baldrige framework, Holliday and other I-SS leaders learned that they had to address the problem of external blame. They also had to create a sense of urgency for change among those staff members who were complacent about mediocre student performance. I-SS leaders learned that facts alone do not change perceptions; nor do fear or force result in lasting change in teachers' beliefs or practices regarding student learning. According to Holliday, "We could tell our staff that over 2,000 children drop out of school every day; however, it does not mean anything until they see a face to go with the dropout statistic."

Three Questions

Early in his tenure, Holliday visited all school sites and hosted staff meetings in each of the school system's communities. At the meetings, he always asked the same three questions:

- What is getting in the way of student learning?

- What do you need to help all children be successful?

- What do you expect from the superintendent?

By asking the first question, about barriers to student learning, Holliday was indirectly letting all staff know the direction in which the school system was moving—toward increasing student learning. He found that the question elicited some people's belief that not all children could learn. "If you do not believe you can reach your destination, then no one will take the trip, much less plan for the trip," he says. It also became clear to Holliday that staff members were prone to blame the lack of student success on external factors. "Apathetic and unmotivated students" was the number-one response to the question, and another frequently cited reason was lack of parental support.

The purpose of the second question, about staff needs, was to align resources to the mission statement, according to Holliday. In response, staff members ranked one of the highest needs as holding children and parents accountable for attendance. It was evident from the student attendance percentage that the school system had a problem in this area, particularly in comparison to other school systems.

The crucial third question—what do you expect from the superintendent?—was intended to help Holliday find out how he could restore trust in the superintendent's position. The responses revealed that the staff wanted the superintendent to be visible, particularly in the schools. They wanted the superintendent to attend student events and be supportive of all programs. They also wanted the superintendent to communicate openly and honestly.

Achieving the Vision

After the meetings, Holliday started tackling school attendance. He created a district leadership team to model an improvement process. "We never called it Baldrige," he says. "We just said we were trying to address a problem that teachers had said was a huge barrier to student learning." Within a year, the school system had improved its attendance rate from one of the lowest in the state to the statewide average. Within three years, I-SS was one of the top-three school systems in the state, and the district maintained that status for the next four years.

The key learning point for Holliday and the other senior leaders was that relationships in the school system had to be repaired for it to move forward. Embarking on a listening tour, including going directly to employees who have direct contact with the most important customers—the students—was the first step toward addressing this need. After that, leaders modeled small behavior changes, starting with the attendance PDSA; they published the early positive results of this effort, thus creating a strong motivator for improvement. "Only after numerous small behavior changes and success did we start to see people reframing their beliefs," says Holliday. "We have gone from having very few staff understand or support our model for continuous improvement to having over 80 percent support."

> "Only after numerous small behavior changes AND success did we start to see people reframing their beliefs. . . . We have gone from having very few staff understand or support our model for continuous improvement to having over 80 percent support."
>
> — Terry Holliday, I-SS Superintendent (2002–2009)

By 2008, when it received the Baldrige Award, I-SS had achieved its vision of performing among the top-ten school systems in North Carolina. At the same time, it maintained a per-pupil expenditure rate that was at least $700 below the state average, ranking it among the bottom-ten school systems in North Carolina for cost. According to Holliday, I-SS achieved these financial results by constantly working to improve the school system's operations; save money in such areas as energy, overtime, and workers' compensation; and reduce costs through improvements in such areas as bus discipline, child nutrition, custodial services, and maintenance services. The system also benefited from collaboration with faith-based and community partners, gaining over $17 million in grant funding over six years.

DOs AND DON'Ts

Don't call it Baldrige (at least at the beginning of your journey). If you are dealing with a community that mistrusts change and innovation based on its experiences, convey the favorable results rather than labeling the improvement methodology.

Don't allow school staff members to give up on children, and don't let students continue to fail until they become dropouts.

Do focus on relationships and building trust among teachers and other school stakeholders. Listen and learn. Then address negative beliefs about and blame for student learning by modeling the change you want to see: model a learning-centered approach and showcase the results it can achieve.

Do create a passion for learning, reigniting this passion among adults. As a school leader, continue to fight the fight.

Response to a Wake-Up Call

Texas Nameplate Company, Inc., is a privately held family business that produces custom nameplates in small, frequent orders primarily for small businesses nationwide and abroad. These identification tags and labels display important usage and safety information for products ranging from high-pressure valves and oil field equipment to computers. Texas Nameplate became a two-time Baldrige Award winner in 2004; the Dallas, Texas-based small business first received this national distinction in 1998—the smallest business ever to be so honored.

Despite the success that led Texas Nameplate to its 1998 Baldrige Award, CEO Dale Crownover says the company soon faced a confidence-shaking crisis—a "wake-up call." "Let 'the wake-up call' be a metaphor for any unexpected event that challenges a company to its core," says Crownover. "Insurance may make you financially whole; but the trust and confidence that is lost may take years to recover."

This insight led Crownover and other Texas Nameplate executives to Lesson 1 of the 12 lessons they cited at a Quest for Excellence conference presentation describing the company's most recent improvement journey: "Always remember where you're coming from. Keeping your responses to the Baldrige Criteria's Organizational Profile [the preface to the Criteria, which asks about your organization and its situation] current and readily accessible is very useful, in good times and bad."

Milestones on a New Journey

Soon after the crisis, Crownover and a senior employee met for a long working lunch and arrived at a two-part vision of the company's future: first, embed the Baldrige Criteria into a company intranet to document progress going forward, and second, embed the next Baldrige Award application into a company intranet to make it easier to chart the organization's progress and apply again.

During the long afternoon talk, the pair raised a number of critical questions for their company but did not try to answer them immediately. "Arriving at our shared vision and knowing the deeper questions involved was the second milestone," says Crownover. "So Lesson 2 is 'Always envision where you want to go and, at the least, begin questioning what you really want by going there.' "

Crownover arrived at a third milestone upon facing reluctance and resistance from some employees who were not enthusiastic about pursuing the Baldrige Award again. Yet Crownover and company "decided not only to break out of the traditional management silo, but also to begin methodically to break down the other silos as well." Lesson 3 was therefore as follows: "Expecting reluctance and resistance, do not retreat into your own silo. Rather, recognize your role as change agent within your organization."

Foundations for Change

Texas Nameplate's fourth lesson—find wise coaches and listen to what they say—was inspired by Crownover's experiences in Baldrige examiner training and service as a judge for the Malcolm Baldrige National Quality Award, through which he refined his knowledge of performance excellence. He found that the annual training sessions "were our fourth milestone, for they inspired us to stay the course in spite of continuing reluctance and resistance to change."

By the end of 2001, Texas Nameplate had implemented The New Hotrod, an intranet-based, embedded Criteria tool that gave Crownover and other employees "a daily systems perspective on our business." The organization soon made significant changes to its information system via more than 25 infrastructure projects. Lesson 5 summed up new learning at that milestone: Know what the pros and the cons are for changing your technology. Go with the pros, and avoid the cons as much as possible.

The organization's sixth milestone on its post-1998 improvement journey was the recognition that traditional management approaches sometimes thwarted its progress toward change. Nonetheless, among the 25-plus projects under way, one significantly shifted the power structure. Called the Just Earning Time and Saving Resources (JETS) program, it was launched to help avoid layoffs while keeping workforce skill levels high during an expected downturn in business after September 11, 2001. Through JETS, Texas Nameplate compensated eligible coworkers with time off for meeting production goals. The success of JETS underscored Lesson 6: Push forward with a commitment to change what you need or want to change.

Success and Trust

Learning the JETS lesson brought Crownover and his company to Lesson 7: Know what "success" means to you and what type of evidence you need to collect to prove to yourselves and others that you've achieved it. Texas Nameplate applied this lesson to a quest for "a way of speaking about success without having to rely on the traditional, bottom-line financial approach." Using the

Baldrige Criteria booklet's scoring guidelines, the company decided on the scoring level it wanted to aim for, converted the descriptors of organizational maturity at that level into eight conditions, and adopted them as its operational definition of "success." Next, the company determined what type of evidence it would collect to see whether it had fulfilled the eight conditions. In particular, the organization collected significant, actionable evidence.

Texas Nameplate's eighth milestone on its improvement journey was incorporating its strategic plan into The New Hotrod: "Beyond revitalizing the strategic planning process itself, we created a Web page so everyone could see the plan at the click of a button." This improvement led Texas Nameplate to Lesson 8: Work with facts made evident through your data collection efforts, and link them to a strategic plan that is constantly displayed.

Texas Nameplate has identified its form of leadership as one of making decisions based on shared insights. For example, the decision to prepare for a 2004 Baldrige Award application was based on senior leaders' insight that doing so would provide many helpful opportunities. Yet Crownover and others found that such "insights were often delayed, if not blocked completely, by hard-to-dispel fears based on unexamined oversights." They also found that behind such oversights was distrust, which may have been the lingering consequence of the company's jolting "wake-up call." Going forward, Crownover and colleagues reminded each other that "Fear is useless; what is needed is trust." Lesson 9 emerged as follows: Facts based on evidence may give you choices, and strategies based on facts and reasoning about them may give you judgments, but when you are making decisions, patiently wait for insights, fearlessly address oversights, and find someone you trust to help you do it.

Texas Nameplate's Lesson 10—trust your coworkers as much as you trust yourselves—follows Lesson 9 closely and also relates to collaborating on a Baldrige application. According to Crownover, his company's executives came to realize that The New Hotrod would be even more effective if they involved coworkers in its development. "We wanted to tell our stories to each other first before we tried to tell them to others in any future Baldrige application. Personal Web pages show how much we trust each other."

The Feedback Report and Beyond

The 11th lesson for Texas Nameplate was simply to stand by its decision to apply for the Baldrige Award. The company found reassurance in knowing that "you literally can't lose in the Baldrige process, because you will get the feedback report whether you win the award or not." Also important to Texas Nameplate was to determine its success in embedding "the Baldrige way" into its business. "It's worth the risk to find out how well you've done it," says Crownover.

Texas Nameplate's final milestone on its improvement journey emerged as employees read the feedback report written by Baldrige examiners. "Certainly, reading about our strengths was confirming and edifying. They 'got it.' And, to be fair, so did we. Reading our 45 opportunities for improvement encouraged us. We will include many of these opportunities in our strategic planning over the next several years."

As the company reached the last milestone of one improvement journey, it approached the first milestone of the next. At the juncture of the two journeys was one final question: "How do we know we are making the right decision?" In response, Crownover put forth his company's Lesson 12: "The telltale sign of knowing you are making the right decision is not whether you are happy with what you have already done along the current journey's level, but whether you are enthusiastically ready to pursue the next level."

Following the 2010 Baldrige Award cycle, Crownover stated, "We did not win Baldrige in 2010 but did receive a site visit. Our goal was obtained. Disappointed we did not win? Not really. Would we have liked to have won? Of course. We received our feedback last month, and it was great. We are already working on the gaps."

"You literally can't lose in the Baldrige process, because you will get the feedback report whether you win the award or not. One should not apply to win the Baldrige Award but to get the feedback and use the information to obtain and sustain high levels of performance."

—Texas Nameplate
CEO Dale Crownover

DOs AND DON'Ts

Don't retreat into a silo when facing resistance from employees about a Baldrige improvement plan. Rather, recognize your role as change agent within your organization.

Don't assume all organizations must strive for the same "success." Instead, determine what level of performance your organization wishes to achieve and what type of evidence you need to collect to prove to yourselves and others that you've achieved it.

Don't let distrust among coworkers deter organizational decision making. Patiently wait for insights and fearlessly address oversights.

Do keep your responses to the Baldrige Criteria's Organizational Profile, which asks questions about your organization and its situation, current and readily accessible in good and bad times.

Do envision where you want to go and, at the least, begin questioning what you really want by going there.

Do make the decision to apply for the Baldrige Award—and recognize that your decision will provide many opportunities to benefit.

Do study the pros and cons of major changes (e.g., in technology), and avoid the cons as much as possible.

Do stay committed to pushing forward with change.

Do reach out to receive training and coaching from Baldrige practitioners.

Do link the collection of organizational performance data with strategic planning.

Do trust your coworkers as much as you trust yourself in preparing a Baldrige Award application.

Do be ready to pursue a new improvement journey even after you receive a Baldrige Award—taking your success to the next level.

The Criteria: Framework for Performance Excellence

The Baldrige Criteria for Performance Excellence are a set of questions in seven interrelated areas (known as categories) that guide you in assessing your organization's performance. For over 20 years, leaders of role-model U.S. organizations in all sectors— manufacturing, service, small business, education, health care, and nonprofit—have used this framework to consider all aspects of running their organizations and to drive improvement. The Criteria help these leaders align processes and resources; improve communication, productivity, and effectiveness; and achieve

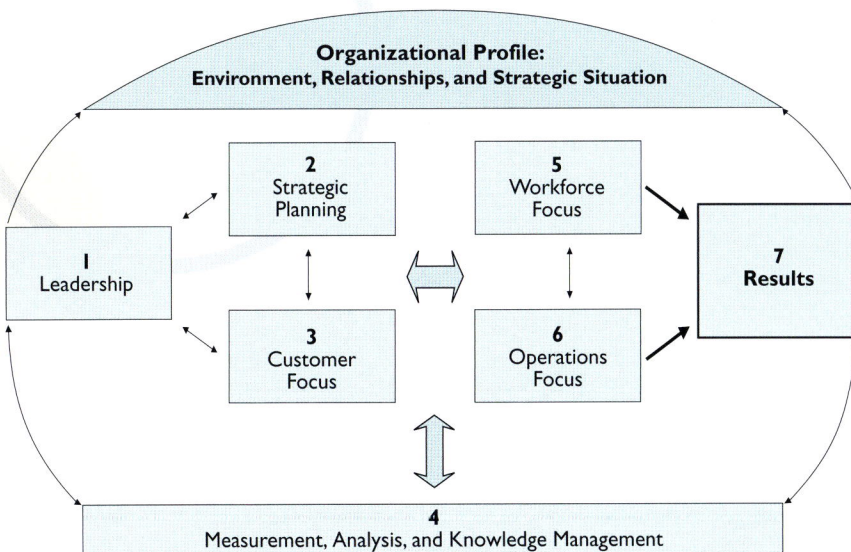

Organizational Profile:
Environment, Relationships, and Strategic Situation

2 Strategic Planning

5 Workforce Focus

1 Leadership

7 Results

3 Customer Focus

6 Operations Focus

4 Measurement, Analysis, and Knowledge Management

strategic goals. Without being prescriptive, the Criteria focus on critical aspects of management that contribute to success.

Responding to the Criteria questions is the beginning of a Baldrige journey toward performance excellence. While answering them fully is not necessarily easy, it will help you see your organization's strengths, opportunities for improvement, and gaps more clearly—so you can move forward with well-informed actions.

Category 1: Leadership

Leadership, the first of the Baldrige framework's seven categories, has two parts—known as "items"—covering senior leadership in the first, and governance and societal responsibilities in the second. The first item asks questions designed to help you examine how your personal actions as an executive guide and sustain your organization. For example,

- **How do senior leaders set your organization's vision and values?**

- **How do senior leaders deploy your organization's vision and values through your leadership system, to the workforce, to key suppliers and partners, and to customers and other stakeholders, as appropriate?**

These questions—like those in all the Criteria categories—are designed to be both timely and timeless. After all, across industries today, leaders must convey their organizations' visions and values in the face of expanding or converging relations with partners, subunits, suppliers, and new stakeholders, and amid mergers, acquisitions, and shifting alliances in the global economy. Additionally, in the education sector, superintendents need to maintain strong partnerships with school boards. And hospital executives must strengthen their partnerships with physicians in order to succeed.

How can the Criteria questions help you? Answering questions such as the ones above will tell you whether you have systematic, effective methods in these areas; whether all employees and work areas use these methods; and whether the methods are integrated with those in other key areas of your organization.

Ethics and Sustainability: The Foundation for Role-Model Results

Visionary leaders embrace the need for ethical behavior and stakeholder trust, understanding that these responsibilities drive and support other results. From surveys on ethical behavior and integrity among management and the workforce, to training on ethics, the tracking of ethical breaches and violations, codes of conduct, and compliance with regulations and standards, Baldrige Award winners look for opportunities to exceed requirements and to excel in areas of legal and ethical behavior. They also contribute to the sustainability of their environmental, social, and economic systems, with approaches to reduce energy usage, emissions, and chemical usage, as well as to recycle waste. In addition, Baldrige Award winners have tracked and surpassed their goals for safety awareness and contributions to the United Way and other community organizations, among other social responsibility measures. Following is a sampling of their results:

- **95% improvement in employees feeling that their management acts with integrity**, according to survey results, over 4 years. This represents an annual improvement of nearly 32%. (CCM, Baldrige Award winner in manufacturing sector)

- **Performance better than the best-in-class benchmark** (Hay companies' 20 high-performing organizations) **for the measure "employee confidence in leadership,"** a 10% overall improvement over 4 years (MEDRAD, Inc., two-time Baldrige Award winner in manufacturing sector)

- **2,300% overall increase in employees attending ethics training** over 4 years (Motorola, Inc., Commercial, Government and Industrial Solutions Sector [CGISS; now Motorola Solutions], Baldrige Award winner in manufacturing sector)

- **95% level of agreement from employees responding to an ethics survey item, "I am expected to maintain a high standard of ethics,"** in the most recent year data were reported (DynMcDermott Petroleum Operations Company [now DM Petroleum Operations Company], Baldrige Award winner in service sector)

- **100% improvement** over 4 years **on its measure of ethical incident occurrences,** improving from an average of 1.5 in 2003 to zero in 2006 (MESA Products, Inc., Baldrige Award winner in small business sector)

- **Steady favorable results on employee perceptions of leadership's ethical behavior,** from a rating of 4.5 out of 5 in 2007 to 4.6 in 2009, according to an annual employee survey (the Center, Baldrige Award winner in nonprofit sector)

- **94% employee rating on leadership's ethics and integrity,** according to survey results, in the most recent year data were reported. That level improved from 91% the previous year. (City of Coral Springs, Baldrige Award winner in nonprofit sector)

- **Sustained low rate of zero to 1 on its measure of fraud or ethics violations by employees** for the 5 years leading up to its Baldrige Award (ARDEC, Baldrige Award winner in nonprofit sector)

- **88% reduction in emissions** over 7 years. In addition, **57% of nonhazardous waste recycled** in the year before it received the Baldrige Award. (Motorola, Inc. CGISS, Baldrige Award winner in manufacturing sector)

- **85% reduction in plate material waste** over 7 years (Clarke American Checks [now Harland Clarke], Baldrige Award winner in manufacturing sector)

- **7% annual improvement in nonmetallic recycling** for 4 years (PRO-TEC, Baldrige Award winner in small business sector)

- **50% reduction in volatile organic compound emissions** over 3 years (Branch-Smith Printing Division, Baldrige Award winner in small business sector)

- **31% reduction in amount of hazardous chemicals and 74% increase in use of environmentally friendly water-based formulations** over 4 years (Stoner, Baldrige Award winner in small business sector)

- **75th percentile in a national Press Ganey comparison on its measure of employee trust in senior leaders** (Heartland Health, Baldrige Award winner in health care sector)

- **Level of 99% or better in common goal of employees completing ethics training** (8 of 11 Baldrige Award winners in the health care sector with this result)

- **100% employees trained on ethical behavior** and **zero violations for Board of Education Ethics Code** in the 5 school years leading up to its Baldrige Award. In addition, **15% reduction in school handbook violations** per 100 students, a 3% improvement per year (I-SS, Baldrige Award winner in education sector)

- **Zero ethical violations for Board of Education Code of Ethics, Student Code of Conduct, and Athlete Code of Conduct.** In addition, **100% compliance record for Special Education and Individuals with Disabilities Act regulations** (Pearl River School District, Baldrige Award winner in education sector)

- **Zero violations or citations of legal, ethical, regulatory, or operational responsibilities** for the five years leading up to its Baldrige Award. In addition, out of 182 U.S. business schools on an EBI student satisfaction survey, Monfort College ranked in the **top 2.5% on both items related to curriculum/teaching of ethics and social responsibility issues.** (Kenneth W. Monfort College of Business, Baldrige Award winner in education sector)

- **Zero violations of the Board of Education Code of Conduct** and **no staff violations of ethical practices as stated in board policy** in at least 18 years (Community Consolidated School District 15, Baldrige Award winner in education sector)

Category 2: Strategic Planning

The Strategic Planning category guides you in examining how your organization develops strategic objectives and action plans, as well as how you implement, change, and measure progress on those objectives and plans. The first item in this category asks how you develop your strategy to address the pressures on your organization and leverage its marketplace advantages. For example,

How do your strategic objectives achieve the following?

- **address your strategic challenges and advantages**

- **address your opportunities for innovation in products, operations, and your business model**

- **capitalize on your current core competencies[1] and address the potential need for new core competencies**

- **balance short- and longer-term challenges and opportunities**

- **consider and balance the needs of all key stakeholders**

- **enhance your ability to adapt to sudden shifts in your market conditions**

Category 3: Customer Focus

The Customer Focus category guides you in examining how your organization engages customers to attain long-term success in the marketplace, including how you listen to the "voice of the customer," build customer relationships, and use customer information to improve and identify opportunities for innovation.

[1] The term "core competencies" refers to your organization's areas of greatest expertise. Your organization's core competencies are those strategically important capabilities that are central to fulfilling your mission or provide an advantage in your marketplace or service environment. Core competencies frequently are challenging for competitors or suppliers and partners to imitate, and they may provide a sustainable competitive advantage. Absence of a needed organizational core competency may result in a significant strategic challenge or disadvantage in the marketplace. Core competencies may involve technology expertise, unique service offerings, a marketplace niche, or a particular business acumen (e.g., business acquisitions).

For example, questions in this category ask how you listen to customers and gain information on their satisfaction and dissatisfaction, how you determine what products to offer and communicate with customers to support them, and how you manage customer relationships and complaints:

- **How do you listen to customers to obtain actionable information?**

- **How do you market, build, and manage relationships with customers to acquire customers and build market share; retain customers, meet their requirements, and exceed their expectations in each stage of the customer life cycle (each stage of their relationship with you); and increase their engagement with you?**

Category 4: Measurement, Analysis, and Knowledge Management

The Measurement, Analysis, and Knowledge Management category examines how you select, gather, analyze, manage, and improve your organization's data, information, and knowledge assets. Other questions focus on how you manage information technology and how you use organizational review findings to improve your organization's performance. For example,

- **How do you select, collect, align, and integrate data and information for tracking daily operations and overall organizational performance, including progress relative to strategic objectives and action plans?**

- **What are your key organizational performance measures, including key short- and longer-term financial measures?**

- **How frequently do you track these measures?**

- **How do you use these data and information to support organizational decision making and innovation?**

Category 5: Workforce Focus

The Workforce Focus category asks how your organization assesses the capabilities and staffing levels you need in your workforce and builds an environment that will lead to high performance by your workforce. Other questions explore your ability to engage, manage, and develop your workforce with the aim of using its full potential in alignment with your mission and strategy. For example,

- **How do you assess your workforce capability and capacity needs, including skills, competencies, and staffing levels?**

- **How does your workforce performance management system support high-performance work and workforce engagement; consider workforce compensation, reward, recognition, and incentive practices; and reinforce a customer and business focus and achievement of your action plans?**

Category 6: Operations Focus

The Operations Focus category (which was the Process Management category until the revised 2011–2012 Criteria) guides you in examining how your organization designs, manages, and improves the systems it uses to accomplish its work, including all external and internal resources. Other questions ask how you design, manage, and improve the key processes you use to implement those work systems in a way that delivers customer value and leads to success and sustainability for your organization. An additional focus is your organization's readiness for emergencies. Here's a sampling of category 6 questions:

- **What are your organization's work systems?**

- **How do you manage and improve your work systems to deliver customer value and achieve organizational success and sustainability?**

Category 7: Results

The Results category guides you in analyzing and reviewing results data and information in all key areas of your organization—product performance and process effectiveness, customers, workforce, leadership and governance, and financial and market performance. Questions focus on your organization's performance relative to that of your competitors and other organizations with similar offerings, as appropriate.

The questions in the first of the five results items ask for data and information on the performance of your organization's key products (including student learning results in education organizations and health care results in health care organizations), as well as process effectiveness and efficiency results. As appropriate, you report your results separately for each of your product offerings, customer groups, market segments, and process types and locations, and include appropriate comparative data. Here are some sample questions:

- **What are your current levels and trends in key measures or indicators of product and process performance that are important to and directly serve your customers?**

- **How do these results compare with the performance of your competitors and other organizations with similar offerings?**

What NOT to do in preparing a Baldrige Award application!

The Dilbert comic strip spoofed the Baldrige Program in the mid-1990s.

Panel 1: I HAVE TO SUBMIT MY PROJECT FOR A "QUALITY" AWARD. I'LL NEED YOUR HELP ON THE DISHONEST PARTS.

Panel 2: THE REAL STORY IS THAT THE PROJECT LOST ITS BUDGET BECAUSE ITS ACRONYM WAS SIMILAR TO A PROJECT THAT WAS CANCELED.

Panel 3: ASSUME YOUR PROJECT WOULD HAVE FAILED AND CLAIM THE SAVINGS FROM AVOIDING IT.

YOU'RE SPOOKY.

E-Mail: SCOTTADAMS@AOL.COM

S. Adams

© 1994 United Feature Syndicate, Inc.

DILBERT: © Scott Adams/Dist. by United Feature Syndicate, Inc.

How Can the Baldrige Program Help You Now?

Integrating the Baldrige Criteria into your organization is not easy or a quick fix. But results show that adopting them can lead to world-class results—from product and process outcomes, to customer-focused outcomes, to workforce-focused outcomes, to leadership and governance outcomes, to financial and market outcomes. But what are the next steps? How can the Criteria help you now?

Self-Assessing

The Baldrige Web site includes many tools that may provide you with insight into your organization's current level of performance and opportunities for improvement. All the tools are free to download and distribute. Here are some examples:

- **Are We Making Progress?** and **Are We Making Progress as Leaders?** are questionnaires for your workforce and leaders that will help you assess your organization's performance and learn what you can improve, as well as focus improvement and communication efforts where your workforce feels they are most needed.

- ***easyInsight*: Take a First Step Toward a Baldrige Self-Assessment** is a questionnaire based on the Baldrige Criteria's Organizational Profile. This self-assessment tool will help you measure your organization against others that have taken the challenge. Then you can identify the gaps in your organization's performance and develop action plans for your journey toward performance excellence.

- The **Organizational Profile** (the preface to the Baldrige Criteria) provides a perfect framework for you to ensure a common understanding about your organization, select information and collect data as you continue your self-assessment, and identify gaps in your approaches and their deployment as a basis for performance improvement efforts.

Applying for Feedback and an Award

Many organizations that have integrated the Criteria for Performance Excellence into their own business models apply for the Malcolm Baldrige National Quality Award, the nation's highest honor for organizational performance given by the President of the United States or one of his direct reports. The organizations featured in this book have all received this honor by using their responses to the Criteria for Performance Excellence as an award application. State and local Baldrige-based programs throughout the country also offer educational services designed for organizations new to Baldrige, and they too have award programs, usually with varied tiers. Many are grouped as part of the Alliance for Performance Excellence, a nonprofit national network that aims to enhance the success and sustainability of organizations. In all award programs, at the local, state, or national levels, award applicants receive feedback reports written by trained examiners that detail the organization's strengths and opportunities for improvement.

Benchmarking Role Models and Sharing Best Practices

Baldrige Award winners are role-model organizations that are ready to share their best practices. On the Baldrige Program's Web site, you can read their success stories and review their Baldrige Award application summaries, which are condensed versions of their actual Baldrige Award applications. Using contact information found on the Baldrige Web site, you can contact the Baldrige Award winners directly for more information on their best management practices and, if applicable, visit them for sharing days and benchmarking. You also can attend presentations by multiple Baldrige Award winners at the annual Quest for Excellence conference held each April in Washington, D.C., and at the fall regional conferences held throughout the United States. Finally, you can listen to online videos on how Baldrige Award winners got started with Baldrige and see portions of their presentations.

Baldrige Award Winners (1998 through 2010)

- 3M Dental Products Division (now known as 3M ESPE Dental Products; 1997)
- ADAC Laboratories (1996)
- Advocate Good Samaritan Hospital (2010)
- Ames Rubber Corporation (1993)
- Armstrong World Industries, Inc., Building Products Operations (1995)
- AT&T Consumer Communications Services (now known as the Consumer Markets Division of AT&T; 1994)
- AT&T Network Systems Group Transmission Systems Business Unit (now part of Alcatel-Lucent; 1992)
- AT&T Universal Card Services (now part of Citigroup, Inc.; 1992)
- AtlantiCare (2009)
- Baptist Hospital, Inc. (2003)
- BI (1999)
- Boeing Aerospace Support (now known as Boeing Support Systems; 2003)
- Boeing Airlift and Tanker Programs (now known as Boeing Global Mobility Systems; 1998)
- Branch-Smith Printing Division (2002)
- Bronson Methodist Hospital (2005)

- Cadillac Motor Car Company (1990)
- Cargill Corn Milling North America (2008)
- Caterpillar Financial Services Corporation-U.S. (2003)
- Chugach School District (2001)
- City of Coral Springs (2007)
- Clarke American Checks, Inc. (now known as Harland Clarke; 2001)
- Community Consolidated School District 15 (2003)
- Corning Incorporated Telecommunications Products Division (1995)
- Custom Research Inc. (now known as GFK Custom Research, Inc.; 1996)
- Dana Commercial Credit Corporation (now part of Dana Holding Corporation; 1996)
- Dana Corporation–Spicer Driveshaft Division (now known as Dana Corporation Torque Traction; 2000)
- DynMcDermott Petroleum Operations Company (now known as DM Petroleum Operations Company; 2005)
- Eastman Chemical Company (1993)
- Federal Express Corporation (1990)
- Freese and Nichols Inc. (2010)
- Globe Metallurgical Inc. (now part of Globe Specialty Metals, Inc.; 1988)
- Granite Rock Company (now known as Graniterock; 1992)
- GTE Directories Corporation (now part of Verizon Information Services; 1994)
- Heartland Health (2009)
- Honeywell Federal Manufacturing & Technologies, L.L.C. (2009)
- IBM Rochester (1990)
- Iredell-Statesville Schools (2008)
- Jenks Public Schools (2005)
- K&N Management (2010)
- KARLEE Company, Inc. (2000)
- Kenneth W. Monfort College of Business (2004)
- Los Alamos National Bank (2000)
- Marlow Industries, Inc. (1991)
- MEDRAD, Inc. (2003 and 2010)
- Mercy Health System (2007)
- Merrill Lynch Credit Corporation (1997)
- MESA Products, Inc. (2006)
- MidwayUSA (2009)
- Milliken & Company (1989)
- Montgomery County Public Schools (2010)
- Motorola Commercial, Government and Industrial Solutions Sector (now part of Motorola Government and Enterprise Mobility Solutions; 2002)
- Motorola, Inc. (1988)

- Nestlé Purina PetCare Company (2010)
- North Mississippi Medical Center (2006)
- Operations Management International, Inc. (now known as CH2M HILL; 2000)
- Pal's Sudden Service (2001)
- Park Place Lexus (2005)
- Pearl River School District (2001)
- Poudre Valley Health System (2008)
- Premier Inc. (2006)
- PRO-TEC Coating Company (2007)
- Richland College (2005)
- Robert Wood Johnson University Hospital Hamilton (2004)
- Saint Luke's Hospital of Kansas City (2003)
- Sharp HealthCare (2007)
- Solar Turbines Incorporated (1998)
- Solectron Corporation (1991 and 1997)
- SSM Health Care (2002)
- STMicroelectronics, Inc.–Region Americas (1999)
- Stoner, Inc. (2003)
- Studer Group (2010)
- Sunny Fresh Foods, Inc. (now known as Cargill Kitchen Solutions; 1999 and 2005)
- Texas Instruments Incorporated Defense Systems & Electronics Group (now part of Raytheon Company; 1992)
- Texas Nameplate Company, Inc. (1998 and 2004)
- The Bama Companies, Inc. (2004)
- The Ritz-Carlton Hotel Company, L.L.C. (now part of Marriott International; 1992 and 1999)
- Trident Precision Manufacturing, Inc. (1996)
- U.S. Army Armament Research, Development and Engineering Center (2007)
- University of Wisconsin-Stout (2001)
- Veterans Affairs Cooperative Studies Program Clinical Research Pharmacy Coordinating Center (2009)
- Wainwright Industries, Inc. (1994)
- Wallace Co., Inc. (1990)
- Westinghouse Electric Corporation Commercial Nuclear Fuel Division (1988)
- Xerox Business Services (1997)
- Xerox Corporation Business Products & Systems (1989)
- Zytec Corporation (now part of Artesyn Technologies; 1991)

For more information, including organizational contacts and locations, profiles, online videos, and Baldrige Award application summaries, visit the Baldrige Performance Excellence Program Web site at http://www.nist.gov/baldrige/.

Appendix: Examples by Criteria Category

The following sampling of Baldrige Award winners' processes and results is provided to exemplify each of the seven Criteria categories. The information and graphics are current as of the year each organization won the Baldrige Award. However, the featured processes and results do not necessarily demonstrate current best practices since organizations that use the Criteria aim to achieve continuous improvements and innovations.

Category 1

Premier Inc., a 2006 Baldrige Award winner, is a role model that has demonstrated its effective and innovative leadership. At the 2007 Quest for Excellence conference, Premier Inc. President and CEO Richard Norling discussed the foundations of his company's visioning process. After recounting how his health care alliance was formed in 1996 through a merger of three smaller alliances, he stressed that "embedding Baldrige was crucial to our shaping Premier successfully from these beginnings."

With a shared purpose of improving the health of communities, Premier Inc. executives set a goal that would extend 20–30 years out. That goal envisioned that the Premier health care alliance's owners (200 or more nonprofit health care providers and health system organizations) would be the highest-quality and most cost-effective health care systems in their markets and that the alliance would become the major influence in reshaping health care. To align the organization with this goal, Premier Inc. leaders set out to ensure that the organization's core roles and strategies would aim toward its achievement and that core values would support it.

Said Norling, "Over the years, and with some great insight from our Baldrige assessment feedback reports, we have put in place an overall leadership system used in common by all our managers. It gives them a common-vocabulary basis for the functions they perform, keeps before us the requirements of leading and managing, and serves as the integrator and summary point of our other main processes." He added that "Baldrige helped us establish what steps, functions, and areas our leadership/management system needs to include in order to meet the Criteria—not only strategic planning, for example, but such things as reward and recognition and organizational learning."

Mercy Health System, a 2007 Baldrige Award winner, provides another example of excellence in leadership. The leaders of the Janesville, Wisconsin-based health care organization demonstrate their personal commitment to the organization's values and serve as role models of those values through Mercy's "servant leadership"

Mercy's Servant Leadership

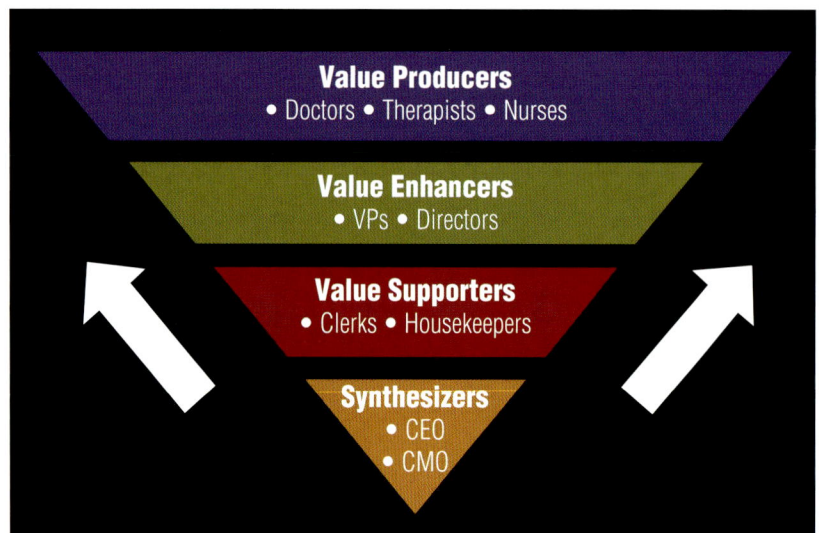

Value Producers
• Doctors • Therapists • Nurses

Value Enhancers
• VPs • Directors

Value Supporters
• Clerks • Housekeepers

Synthesizers
• CEO
• CMO

(depicted in the graphic on page 100). This approach inverts the traditional, top-down management style such that organizational leaders become facilitators who serve the workforce, whose members, in turn, provide value to patients and other stakeholders. To ensure that the entire organization uses servant leadership consistently, Mercy's leaders are trained on the philosophy at the Mercy Institute for Leadership Excellence and the Leadership Development Academy.

Veterans Affairs Cooperative Studies Program Clinical Research Pharmacy Coordinating Center, which received the Baldrige Award in 2009, also demonstrates excellence in leadership. One way executives of the Albuquerque, New Mexico-based organization personally promote legal and ethical behavior is through a popular course taken by the entire workforce: "The Code of the West: Ethics the Cowboy Way." The Cowboy Ethics Program sets behavioral expectations for employees and conveys them through beliefs such as "live each day with courage; take pride in your work; be tough, but fair; and ride for the brand."

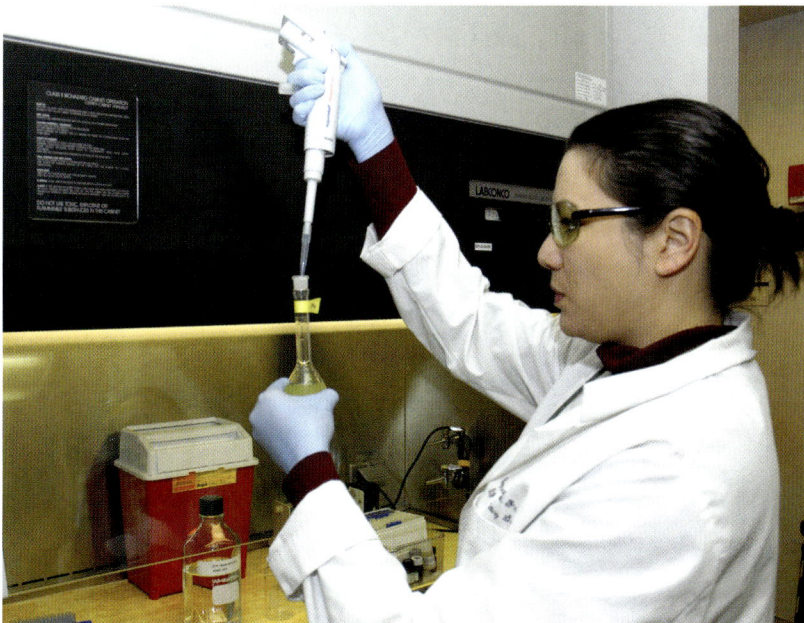

As another example of role-model leadership, **Nestlé Purina PetCare Company**, a 2010 Baldrige Award winner in manufacturing, has established its vision and values based on four principles of the company's founder: "Stand Tall, Think Tall, Smile Tall, and Live Tall."

Senior leaders of the St. Louis, Missouri-based company have added a "5th Tall": "We create tall with innovation." They communicate these ideals through many means and ensure that they are integrated with company strengths and processes, including employee recruitment and hiring.

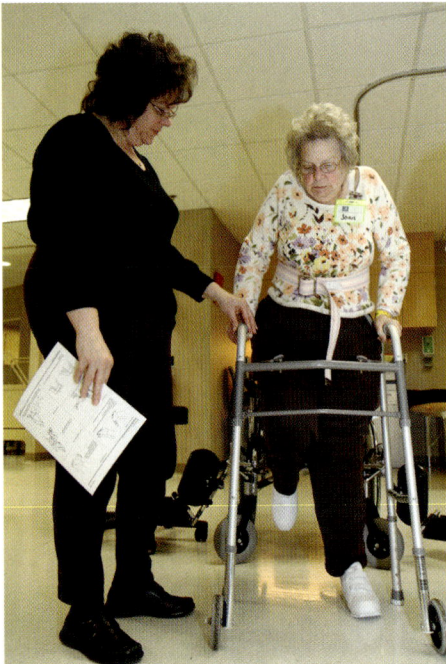

Heartland Health, a 2009 Baldrige Award winner, demonstrates excellence in leadership and social responsibility in its vision of and commitment to community health. Based in St. Joseph, Missouri, this nonprofit, community-based integrated health system has developed a three-tiered, collaborative approach to improving the health of the residents of the Missouri, Kansas, Nebraska, and Iowa communities it serves. This approach is visualized as a pyramid of three layers that illustrates how the organization's entities work together to accomplish a common vision of making Heartland Health and its service areas the best and safest places in America where people can receive health care and live a healthy and productive life. This vision is maintained in plain sight through its integration at all four entities of the organization: Heartland Regional Medical Center, Heartland Clinic, Community Health Improvement Solutions, and Heartland Foundation. Heartland Health participates in a community-wide planning process that addresses seven areas of public health: healthy kids, deliberate safety, healthy/active elderly, community-wide mental health, optimal cost and access to health care, healthy lifestyles, and health management. This approach has led to the development of initiatives such as emPowerU, a state-of-the-art technology learning center managed by Heartland Health's foundation that offers programs to support youth and promote community health.

Category 2

2007 Baldrige Award winner **City of Coral Springs,** Florida, has demonstrated excellence in strategic planning by involving all citizens, including business owners, in creating a shared vision for the future. Coral Springs gathers input from citizens through a citywide annual survey, focus groups, transaction surveys, an automated comment-and-complaint system, the City Hall in the Mall, advisory boards and committees, community visioning forums,

Coral Springs' Strategic Planning

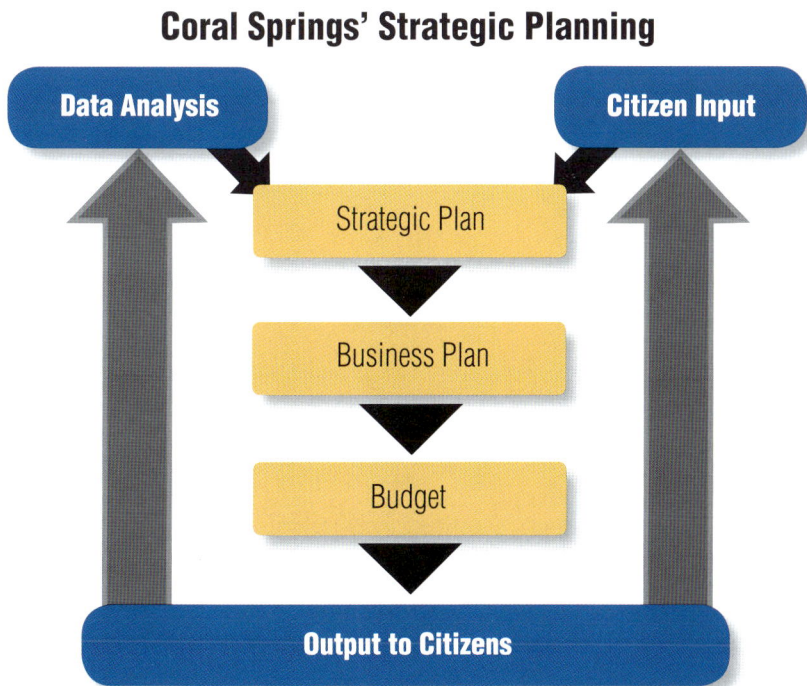

Data Analysis → Strategic Plan → Business Plan → Budget → Output to Citizens ← Citizen Input

and annual "Slice of the Springs" meetings. Based on input from these forums and on key environmental and performance data, the city establishes the strategic plan, which includes strategic priorities, directional statements, goals, core values, and key measures of intended outcomes. As illustrated in the figure on the previous page, the strategic plan, in turn, drives the city's operational plan, its budgets, and the services it provides to citizens, who then give feedback that becomes input for the next planning process.

Freese and Nichols Inc., a 2010 Baldrige Award winner in the small business category, also demonstrates strategic planning excellence. The multiservice engineering, architecture, and environmental science consulting firm uses a year-long strategic planning process to identify indicators in key focus areas, as well as critical actions and measures, for its balanced scorecard. Representatives from all areas of the organization participate in the process. And a management-level Futures Committee examines trends and changes that are likely to impact the firm in five to 15 years. In addition, the firm uses a "catch-ball" process to cascade plans down to the individual level within the organization in order to ensure a commitment of resources to carry out the planned strategies.

Freese and Nichols's Annual Strategic Planning Process

Establish Strategic Direction	External Scan	Strategic Imperative	Revised Mission/ Vision/Guiding Principles	Market Scan
Develop Strategies and Plans	Market & Service Strategies	Growth Strategies	Capability Strategies	Goals and Actions
Deploy Strategies and Plans	Freese and Nichols Inc. Planning Retreat	Group Annual Operating Plan Retreats	Annual Operating Plan Budget	Individual Dev. Plans

2010 Baldrige Award winner **Montgomery County Public Schools (MCPS)** provides another example of excellence in strategic planning. This excellence is seen in the systematic alignment of the strategic plan, Our Call to Action: Pursuit of Excellence (OCA), with actions at every level of the school system. The OCA, rooted in the school district's vision, mission, values, goals, and academic priorities, also aligns with the Maryland State Board of Education's master plan and federal education requirements. The plan reflects the shared concerns and expectations of the district's partners, customers, and community members as a result of senior leaders' extensive outreach efforts to them. And the plan cascades downward such that each office, department, and school in the 144,000-student system has developed related improvement plans and performance measures. The well-aligned plans enable the suburban D.C. school district to develop and deliver rigorous instruction that meets students' individual needs.

Category 3

Ritz-Carlton Hotel Company, a 1992 and 1999 Baldrige Award winner, demonstrates excellence in customer focus. The company's Customer Loyalty and Satisfaction System (C.L.A.S.S.; depicted in the figure below) and the Mystique system developed in more recent years, for example, have enabled Ritz-Carlton to remember the individual service preferences of hundreds of thousands of guests by documenting and storing information on guests' likes and dislikes in a database. Such approaches have allowed the company's workforce and suppliers to know what is distinctive about each customer or event at the Ritz-Carlton's hotels. Former Ritz-Carlton Vice President of Operations John Timmerman has noted that, through processes like C.L.A.S.S., the Ritz-Carlton can adjust its offerings to changes such as the less formal style of service now required by many customers.

Ritz-Carlton's C.L.A.S.S.

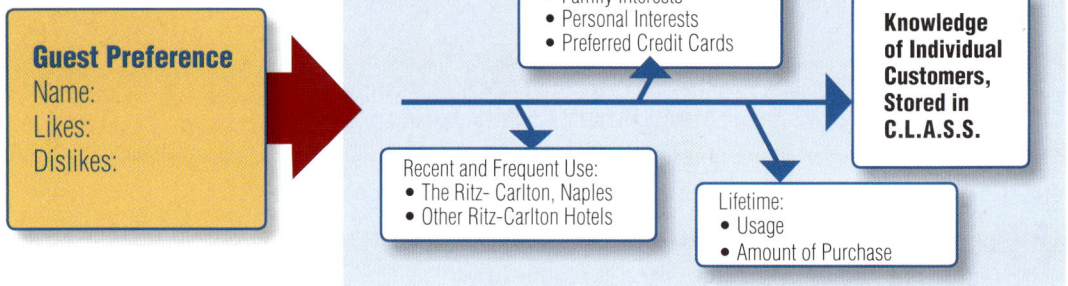

Guest Preference
Name:
Likes:
Dislikes:

- Likes/Dislikes
- Previous Difficulties
- Family Interests
- Personal Interests
- Preferred Credit Cards

Knowledge of Individual Customers, Stored in C.L.A.S.S.

Recent and Frequent Use:
- The Ritz- Carlton, Naples
- Other Ritz-Carlton Hotels

Lifetime:
- Usage
- Amount of Purchase

AtlantiCare, a 2009 Baldrige Award winner, is also a role model in its focus on customers. Through a five-phase, voice-of-the-customer inquiry process, the southeastern New Jersey health care provider gathers the needs and preferences of its patients and other stakeholders. AtlantiCare uses this input to identify health care services and innovations that will satisfy customers. Information from focus groups held

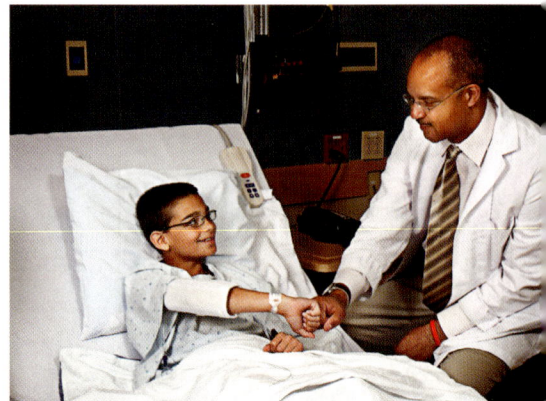

by AtlantiCare led to the development of the Access Center, a multilingual telephone information service for the community that includes a 24-hour, Web-based, self-service feature. The Access Center met patients' need for expanded access to AtlantiCare and helped them navigate the health care system. A measure of the Access Center's success is that the number of returning callers tripled from 2006 to 2008.

2007 Baldrige Award winner **Sharp HealthCare** also exemplifies excellence in customer focus. Through the Customer Knowledge System and multiple ways of listening to the voice of the customer, the San Diego, California-based health care organization systematically identifies, considers, and takes action to meet customer needs and preferences. Sharp's workforce is empowered to use a wide range of tools to identify the needs, expectations, and preferences of former, current, and potential customers and partners at all levels. This information is integrated into Sharp's strategic planning, goal setting, program development, work process redesign, selection of technology, and consumer marketing.

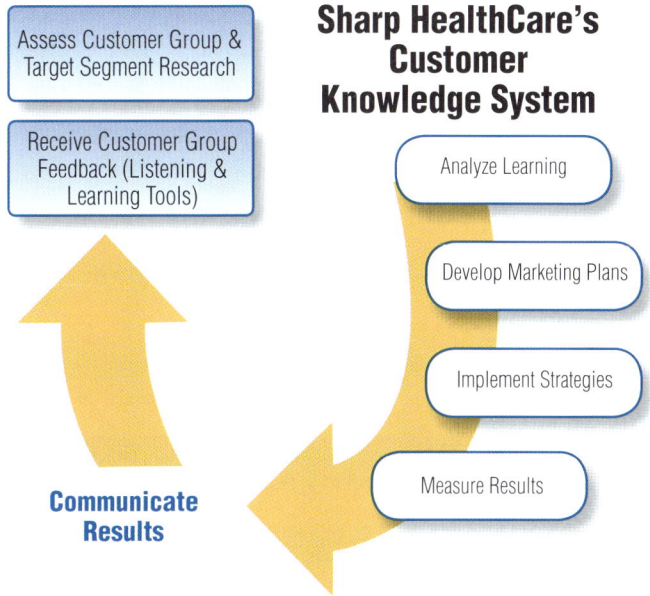

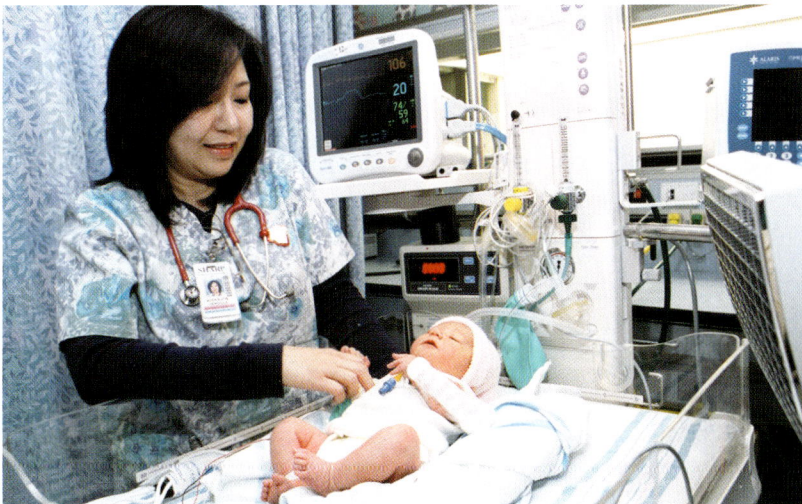

Sharp HealthCare's Customer Knowledge System

- Assess Customer Group & Target Segment Research
- Receive Customer Group Feedback (Listening & Learning Tools)
- Analyze Learning
- Develop Marketing Plans
- Implement Strategies
- Measure Results
- **Communicate Results**

Category 4

Texas Nameplate Company, Inc., a Baldrige Award winner in 1998 and 2004, demonstrates excellence in measurement, analysis, and knowledge management. This small business has used customized software (including Simon™, Real-Time Dashboard™, and Pipeline Dashboard™) on a Web-browser-based intranet known as The New Hotrod to share and analyze data in support of decision making and innovation. On The New Hotrod, the company documents the "facts" of its business in Web pages that are constantly updated with real-time information, and employees may maintain their own Web pages to share information. The company refines its work processes as the significance of data becomes apparent. For Texas Nameplate, the results of this effective management of organizational knowledge have been innovation and improved integration.

Texas Nameplate's The New Hotrod

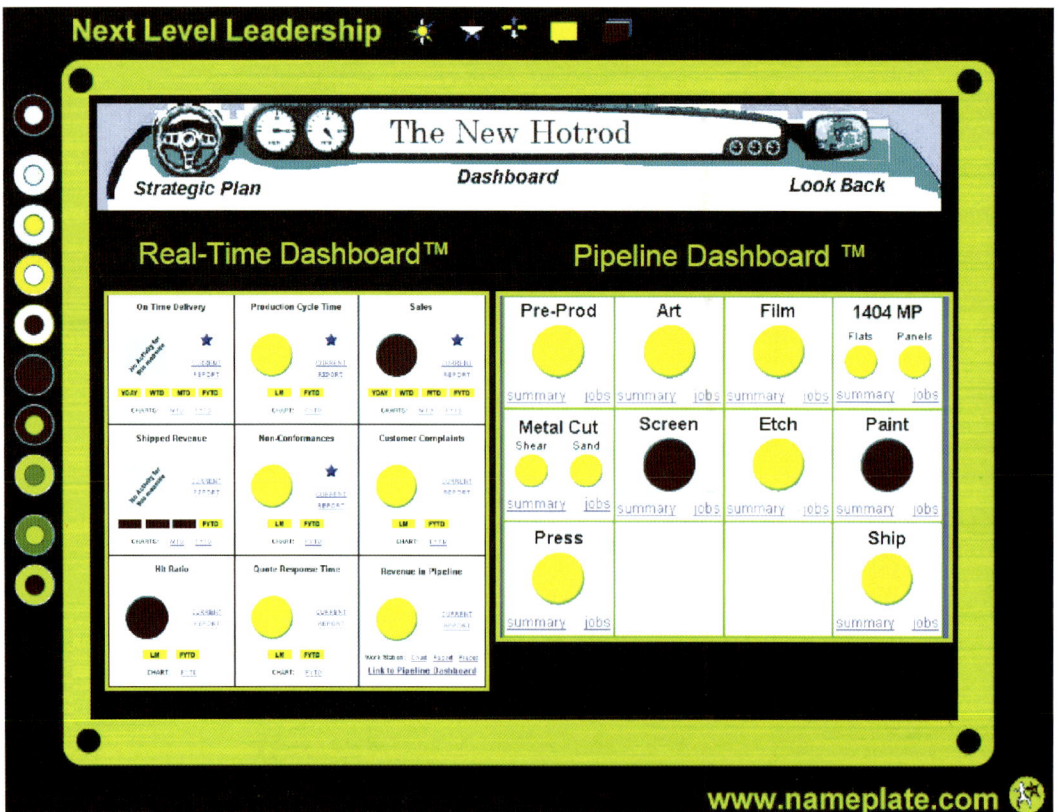

2007 Baldrige Award winner **U.S. Army Armament Research, Development and Engineering Center (ARDEC)** has demonstrated excellence in its consistent use of fact-based decision making. As illustrated in the figure below, ARDEC assembles and transfers relevant knowledge for use in strategic planning through its Performance Assurance System. With this system, ARDEC ensures that its performance is aligned with and supports its overall strategy. Employees at each of the organization's directorates gather competitive and comparative data during strategic planning. ARDEC uses these data to ensure that it remains the most innovative supplier of armament solutions while meeting its customers' requirements for cost, schedule, and performance.

ARDEC's Performance Assurance System

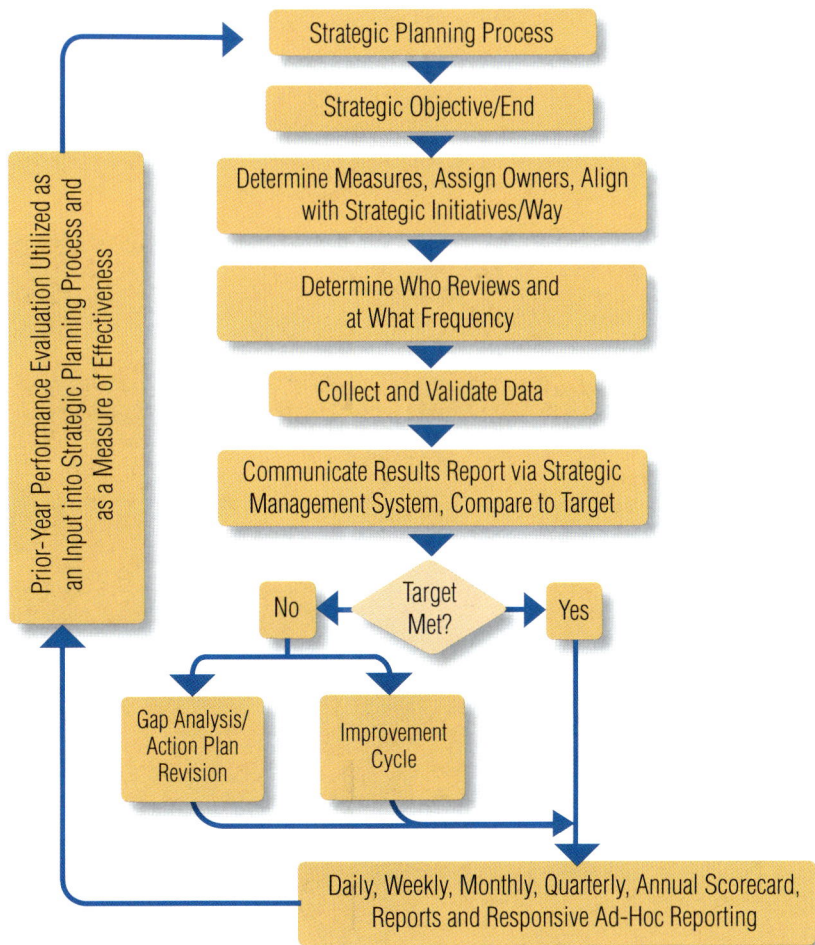

Strategic Planning Process

Strategic Objective/End

Determine Measures, Assign Owners, Align with Strategic Initiatives/Way

Determine Who Reviews and at What Frequency

Collect and Validate Data

Communicate Results Report via Strategic Management System, Compare to Target

Target Met?

No → Yes

Prior-Year Performance Evaluation Utilized as an Input into Strategic Planning Process and as a Measure of Effectiveness

Gap Analysis/Action Plan Revision

Improvement Cycle

Daily, Weekly, Monthly, Quarterly, Annual Scorecard, Reports and Responsive Ad-Hoc Reporting

Category 5

2009 Baldrige Award winner **Honeywell Federal Manufacturing & Technologies, L.L.C. (FM&T)** has modeled excellence in its workforce focus. The management and operating contractor of a National Nuclear Security Administration plant in Kansas City, Missouri, among other contract locations, has a workforce of 2,704. They serve government and private-sector clients in multidisciplinary engineering and manufacturing operations. Through the Enterprise Alignment Process, the company links the daily accountability of its salaried and hourly employees to its balanced scorecard of performance measures and its strategic plan. The result has been high levels of employee satisfaction as measured by survey scores. Seventy-two percent of the company's employees agreed that they felt appreciated, and 81 percent agreed that management listened to their ideas. In addition, 72 percent were satisfied with the positive environment, and 80 percent were satisfied with the information provided to them. In all of these areas, FM&T's workforce had higher satisfaction survey scores than the organization's competitors, who are best-in-class commercial manufacturers.

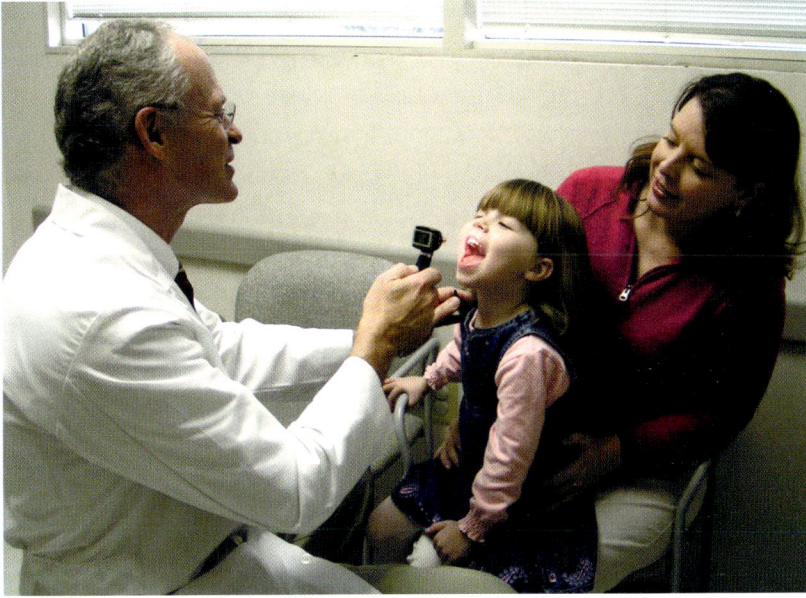

2007 Baldrige Award winner **Mercy Health System** has also demonstrated excellence in workforce focus. The health care organization's commitment to engaging and satisfying workforce members, who are called "partners," is conveyed through its three-pronged approach: inform, involve, and celebrate. As part of "inform," the Mercy Leadership Group communicates in ways that ensure that the workforce knows the organization's goals, understands them, and, most important, can relate them to Mercy's mission: to provide exceptional health care services that result in healing in the broadest sense. For the "involve" prong, Mercy forms a partnership with its workforce. For example, the organization administers annual satisfaction surveys to learn what is most important to employees; conducts focus groups on diversity, wellness, and safety; and involves the workforce in developing action plans. As part of "celebrate," programs such as the Culture of Excellence ensure that workforce members achieve personal and organizational success. To determine the factors that affect workforce engagement and satisfaction, the Culture of Excellence Steering Committee and the Human Resource Planning Committee analyze employee feedback and other data. The organization celebrates people, ideas, and achievements with recognition dinners, "baskets for champions," and the Partner Idea Program, which has rewarded over $15,000 in cash prizes to workforce members who submit ideas.

Another Baldrige role model, **MEDRAD, Inc.,** which received the Baldrige Award in 2003 and again in 2010, has greatly benefitted from engaging its employees in organizational improvement. Participation in MEDRAD's Value Improvement Program, which captures, measures, tracks, and recognizes employees' ideas for improvement, has increased 12-fold from 50 employees in 1999 to more than 600 in 2009. Value delivered from the program has increased from $23,000 per employee in 2005 to $45,000 in 2009, dramatically surpassing *Industry Week* magazine's "Best Plant" benchmark level of $10,000 per employee for similar improvement programs.

Category 6

Boeing Airlift and Tanker Programs, a 1998 Baldrige Award winner now known as Boeing Mobility, has demonstrated excellence in designing, managing, and improving its work processes. As a subunit of the Boeing Company, with headquarters in Long Beach, California, the manufacturer created a seven-step approach to defining, managing, stabilizing, and improving its work processes. This process-based management, or PBM, helped the company continually improve the design, development, and production of the C-17 Globemaster 11 airlifter for its primary customer, the U.S. Air Force. The company also used PBM to set measures of quality, timeliness, and cycle time—which serve as indicators of efficiency and are the chief drivers of customer satisfaction for the company.

2009 Baldrige Award winner **MidwayUSA,** a small business with two facilities in Columbia, Missouri, is another role model in how it designs, manages, and improves its work processes to deliver value to customers. The Internet and catalog retail merchant of shooting, reloading, gunsmithing, and hunting products uses 1,500 documented processes to run the business. Every one of these processes focuses on a key stakeholder.

The strong focus on operations demonstrated by **DynMcDermott Petroleum Operations Company** (**DM**; now DM Petroleum Operations Company), which received the Baldrige Award in 2005, has delivered value to its customer, the U.S. Department of Energy (DOE), and boosted organizational success and sustainability in partnership with the DOE. DM determines the requirements for its key value creation processes (see figure below) in collaboration with its customer. If the DOE's mission requirements, orders, or strategic plan changes, DM incorporates those changes into its strategic plan and implements them through related action plans. Changes in the needs of customers, suppliers, and stakeholders are incorporated in real time through daily communications and from weekly, monthly, quarterly, and six-month reviews. All processes incorporate customer feedback, and many incorporate supplier feedback, such as input on security and emergency preparedness.

DM's Key Value Creation Processes

- Crude Oil Acquisition (Fill Process)

- Drawdown Process

- Vapor Pressure

- Crude Oil Quality

- Maintenance Process

- Cavern Integrity

- Emergency Preparedness Process

- ISO 14001 Process (Environmental)

Category 7

Boeing Airlift and Tanker Programs (now known as Boeing Mobility) achieved excellent results, including a 54 percent reduction over five years in time spent on rework and repair of the C-17. In addition, the mean time between corrective maintenance procedures increased eightfold between 1993 and 1997, and when the Boeing subunit received the Baldrige Award in 1998, the C-17's level of performance was nearly four times better than that of the next best competitor's aircraft. Boeing attributed these results to quality improvements and efficiencies achieved through its systematic methodology for managing its manufacturing and other processes.

Ritz-Carlton Hotel Company's extraordinary customer focus has paid off in customer satisfaction and financial gains. In a survey of frequent leisure travelers, Ritz-Carlton held the top score in complete satisfaction during the period leading up to its second Baldrige Award. Its closest competitor's score was 14 percentage points lower. The company's return on investment increased 85 percent over three years. Revenue per available room exceeded the industry average by more than 300 percent—and the upscale hotel group average by more than 150 percent. In turn, its gross profit increased more than 12 percent over three years. Ritz-Carlton also managed to decrease employee turnover nearly 60 percent over the nine years leading up to its 1999 Baldrige recognition. Its turnover rate was more than

20 percentage points lower than the industry average at the time. At 77 percent, employee satisfaction on all issues surveyed was 23 percentage points higher than the service company norm.

2007 Baldrige Award winner **Sharp HealthCare** led the San Diego region in consumers' perception of quality (see the figure below) as a result of efforts to listen to the voice of the customer and respond to the community's requirements. In addition, Sharp's focus on enhancing customer relationships and loyalty led to sustained improvement in both inpatient and outpatient loyalty to and likelihood of recommending Sharp. In these areas, ratings of Sharp either approached or met the 75th percentile for hospitals tracked by Press Ganey, as shown in the figure on the next page.

Sharp HealthCare's Patient Perception of Quality

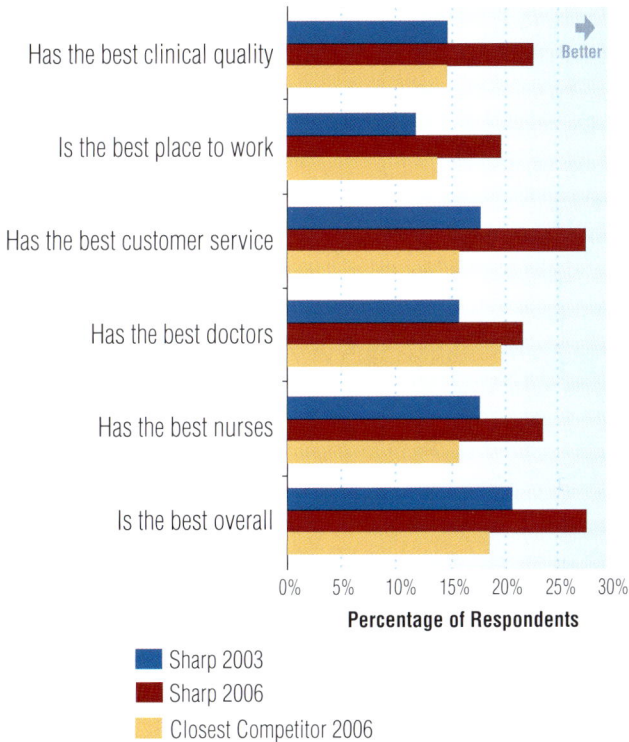

Percentage of Respondents

- Sharp 2003
- Sharp 2006
- Closest Competitor 2006

Sharp HealthCare's Patient Loyalty and Likelihood to Recommend

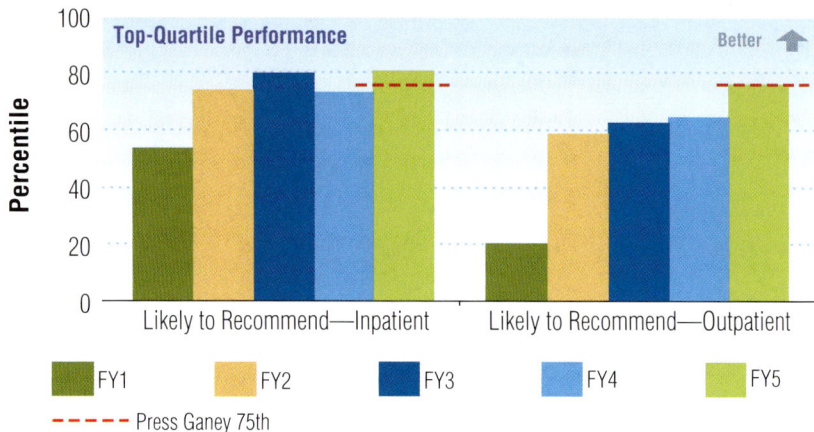

Chart: Percentile (y-axis, 0 to 100) showing "Likely to Recommend—Inpatient" and "Likely to Recommend—Outpatient" with Top-Quartile Performance and Better indicator

Legend: FY1, FY2, FY3, FY4, FY5, ----- Press Ganey 75th

For 2005 Baldrige Award winner **DynMcDermott Petroleum Operations Company** (**DM**; now DM Petroleum Operations Company), the measure of drawdown readiness (displayed in the figure below) shows how effective process management enables the organization to meet customer requirements. DM's first priority is operational readiness because, in the event of an interruption to the nation's oil supply and an order from the President of the United States, the Strategic Petroleum Reserve must distribute crude oil to refineries. Called "drawdown," this is DM's primary mission. Over the decade preceding 2005, DM continually improved its Operational Readiness System, a strategic planning and organizational tool to ensure efficient, secure, and safe drawdown and fill. DM's organizational approach has worked well; between 2001 and 2005, DM's drawdown system was available 98 percent of the time or more. In each year and at each site, the system exceeded the DOE's expectations.

DM's Drawdown Readiness

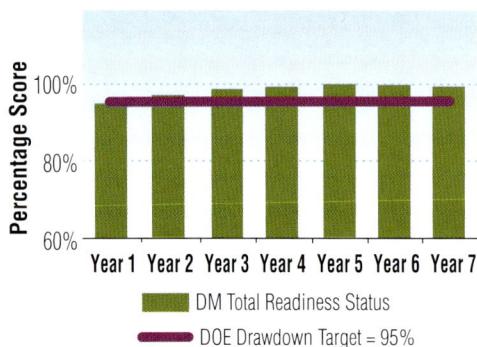

Chart: Percentage Score (y-axis, 60% to 100%) for Year 1 through Year 7

Legend: DM Total Readiness Status, DOE Drawdown Target = 95%

In 2005, DM's responses to Hurricanes Katrina and Rita demonstrated the company's systematic approaches to operational readiness, emergency planning, and emergency response. Although both hurricanes affected several company sites, displacing employees, DM restored oil operations, processes, and data communication systems within five days; in response to the President's drawdown order, DM delivered approximately 30 million barrels of oil without incident.